Cultural Perspectives in Video Game Audio

Cultural Perspectives in Video Game Audio explores the fundamental role of sound – specifically sound effects, music, and voice acting – in video games. This book provides readers with a deeper understanding of the impact of sound on gameplay and storytelling and examines sound's potential to either preserve or diminish cultural diversity.

Organised into six chapters, this book examines various aspects of audio and its cultural implications, offering readers insights into the vital role sound plays in video game design and player experience from a new perspective. It delves into a wide range of topics, including natural soundscapes; the interplay between human activities and their environments; linguistic elements which express cultural identity; the role of non-verbal audio in video games; musical preferences and structures; and the use of sound symbols as expressions of cultural identity.

Cultural Perspectives in Video Game Audio is a valuable resource for researchers and students in fields such as sound design, game studies, and media studies, as well as sound anthropologists and ethnomusicologists. It will also be of interest to game sound designers and developers seeking to create more culturally authentic soundscapes for their audiences.

Mohammad R. Azadehfar is a professor in Ethnomusicology at Tehran Art University. He has received five grants for music multidisciplinary studies from University of London, University of the Arts, and the Iran National Science Foundation (INSF). Azadehfar won the biannual book prize for *Melodic Structure in Iranian Music* from INMH in 2019.

Cultural Perspectives in Video Game Audio

Mohammad R. Azadehfar

Routledge
Taylor & Francis Group
LONDON AND NEW YORK

Designed cover image: Nazanin Farshbaf

First published 2026
by Routledge
4 Park Square, Milton Park, Abingdon, Oxon OX14 4RN

and by Routledge
605 Third Avenue, New York, NY 10158

Routledge is an imprint of the Taylor & Francis Group, an informa business

British Library Cataloguing-in-Publication Data
A catalogue record for this book is available from the British Library

ISBN: 978-1-032-96946-6 (hbk)
ISBN: 978-1-032-96945-9 (pbk)
ISBN: 978-1-003-59139-9 (ebk)

DOI: 10.4324/9781003591399

Typeset in Sabon
by Apex CoVantage, LLC

Contents

Preface

In an increasingly interconnected world, globalisation presents both opportunities and challenges. While it fosters global exchange, it can also homogenise cultures, leading to a loss of unique identities. This book delves into the critical role of audio in video games, exploring how it can either preserve or erode cultural diversity.

The tendency towards cultural homogenisation has been observed within various media industries, including the influential system of mainstream American cinema, often referred to as "Hollywood." While Hollywood can signify a geographic location, this book primarily employs the term to denote the industrial production model and associated aesthetic conventions that have dominated global cinema. As Bordwell and Thompson (2012) outline, this system prioritises narrative clarity, broad audience appeal, and commercial success, which can sometimes lead to a reduction of cultural specificity. However, it is vital to acknowledge that the relationship between cinema and video games is not a simple linear progression. Video games possess distinct ludic qualities, interactive mechanics, and diverse development ecosystems that differentiate them from cinematic experiences.

Nevertheless, the influence of mainstream cinematic practices, particularly the drive for widespread appeal, has contributed to a tendency towards homogenised narratives and soundscapes in some video games. This homogenisation, driven by market demands, often prioritises familiarity over authenticity, resulting in soundscapes that lack cultural depth and resonance. This can lead to experiences that feel familiar yet ultimately lack a strong sense of place or cultural identity.

Video games, as a dominant form of entertainment, hold immense potential to celebrate cultural diversity. My goal in writing this book is to emphasise the importance of preserving cultural diversity in video game audio, advocating for an approach that honours and celebrates the vast array of cultures that enrich our world.

Soundscapes, musical compositions, and auditory cues are essential in immersing players in virtual worlds, evoking emotions, and enhancing narrative depth. In this volume, I invite readers to join in rethinking the role of audio in video games through a cultural lens – one that prioritises understanding over recognition. By illuminating the unseen threads that bind sound and culture, we can appreciate video game audio not just as a functional component but as a vital part of a larger conversation about identity, experience, and expression in the digital age.

This book explores how audio operates as a cultural phenomenon in video games, reflecting social values, fostering community identities, and challenging normative narratives, while consciously refraining from focusing on specific games in the market. This approach is not a dismissal of established titles or a lack of appreciation for their contributions, but rather a deliberate strategy to elevate the discussion beyond individual case studies.

By avoiding focusing on commercial examples, we can delve deeper into the broader cultural contexts that shape and are shaped by video game audio. Since video games are interactive in nature and require player's consistence participation to progress, I have chosen to leave the exemplifying part for the reader to complete. This allows you to draw your own connections between the concepts discussed and your favourite games and fosters a deeper understanding of the profound impact of sound on culture and society.

The chapters that follow are structured to guide the reader through the utility of video game audio in its cultural context, beginning with foundational concepts of geophony and biophony and moving beyond to anthropophony, the soundscape crafted by human activity. Each chapter delves deeper into the sonic landscape, examining how sounds shape our realities, influence our emotions, and communicate meanings often lost in verbal language. The interplay of language, music, and sound symbolism not only enriches our communication in video games but also serves as a mirror reflecting the diversity of human experience to illuminate the pivotal role that sound plays in our understanding of culture and society.

It is crucial to acknowledge the hierarchical structure within game development, particularly regarding audio implementation. While this book explores the cultural specification of sound and their potential application in games, it is essential to clarify that the creative vision, primarily driven by the game director, dictates the fundamental soundscape. The sound team's role, therefore, is to execute that vision with precision and artistry. For instance, the presence of a dragon or ants in a game is rarely a sound designer's independent choice; rather, it reflects the director's narrative and aesthetic goals. Consequently, the focus shifts from whether to include certain sounds to *how* those sounds are crafted to effectively convey the director's intent. This involves not only technical proficiency but also a deep understanding of the desired emotional impact within its cultural interpretations. Furthermore, the collaborative nature of game development, where creative directors lead the thematic direction, emphasises that sound design is a service to a larger, unified artistic vision.

I hope that examining the intersection of culture and sound in gaming will inspire developers, creators, and players to celebrate the richness of our multifaceted cultural heritage, rather than succumb to the temptation of a sanitised, one-size-fits-all model.

Acknowledgements

I would like to express my heartfelt gratitude to all those who have supported and guided me throughout the years of writing this monograph.

My sincere appreciation goes to my colleagues, whose constructive feedback and engaging discussions significantly enriched my research. The collaborative spirit and solidarity we shared made this process both enjoyable and enlightening. I am also deeply grateful to my research assistants – Nasim Taghipour, Zahra Shahparast, Saba Esmaili, and Sara Shahlai – for their invaluable help in data collection and their various contributions to the preparation of this book.

A special thanks is due to the staff at Routledge, particularly the audio and music editors, for their exceptional support in facilitating the publication of my research. Your commitment to advancing scholarly work is truly commendable.

Finally, I would like to express my deepest gratitude to my family for their unwavering support during this study. Their generous input, both in form and intellectual content, has been instrumental in shaping this work.

I would like to acknowledge the broader academic community whose works have inspired me and laid the groundwork for this monograph. I hope that this contribution will add to the ongoing discourse in the field.

Introduction and Preliminary Concepts

Introduction

Storytelling has been with us since the earliest days of humanity. We wove stories in our minds long before language, through daydreams, by imagination, and the fantastical landscapes of our nightdreams. "A society is composed of fractious people with different personalities, goals, and agendas. What connects us beyond our kinship ties? Story" (Gottschall, 2012, p. 110). From the earliest societies, this storytelling impulse manifested in diverse forms – theatrical performances, sung epics, and countless other variations. With the advancement of technology, our storytelling tools have also transformed – from the enchanting art of cinema to the captivating realms of animation and the interactive experiences of digital multimedia. Throughout this journey, storytellers have strived to captivate their audiences, weaving narratives that boost our imaginations and transport us to new worlds.

This same desire for engagement extends beyond stories. Humans are drawn to the challenge, a natural disposition evident from our earliest years. Video games brilliantly combine the power of storytelling with the thrill of competition. This effective mix – immersive narratives intertwined with stimulating challenges – lies at the heart of the immense popularity of video games.

The explosive growth of any media inevitably fuels the industry behind it. This expansion fosters an environment that encourages innovation, leading to an increased quantity and, ideally, quality of products for consumers. However, this industrialisation can also pose challenges. One such concern is so-called "cultural imperialism," where dominant cultural elements are imposed on a broader audience. This homogenisation risks flattening the rich rainbow of the colourful cultures on different continents. We can see this dynamic at play in the film industry, where Hollywood cinema has cast a long shadow over local film traditions. The resistance of European film industries in countries like Italy and Spain, as well as Asian cinema trades like India, Japan, and Iran, to the overshadowing influence of Hollywood, highlights these concerns about American cultural dominance. A less diverse world, devoid of vibrant cultural experiences, could be detrimental for everyone, including Americans themselves.

DOI: 10.4324/9781003591399-1

In video games, sound is not just background noise. It is an influential world-builder. From the triumphant swells of victory music to the unsettling creaks of a haunted house, soundtracks evoke emotions and atmospheres that can make you feel happy, scared, or anything in between. They transport us to different cultures, amplify the tension in a boss fight, and even foster a sense of community through recognisable character voices. Sound is a vital tool for game designers to shape cultural experiences within the digital realm. In this volume, I aim to empower video game designers and developers to create more authentic cultural experiences for their audiences. To achieve this, I will explore various anthropological concepts related to sound and present them in a clear, practical way for direct application in video game design.

Globalisation vs. Internationalisation

Globalisation refers to the process of creating a video game that has universal appeal and can be played by players from different countries regardless of their cultural backgrounds. "Globalization is often presented as the strategic effort to treat the world, or a significant part of it, as a single market in which to do business" (Tallman & Fladmoe-Lindquist, 2002, p. 116). This may involve incorporating themes, characters, and gameplay mechanics that resonate with a broad audience, avoiding cultural references and stereotypes that may be offensive or incomprehensible to players from other regions, and ensuring that the game is not overly reliant on language or cultural-specific jokes or nuances. Even though globalised games require understanding and respecting cultural differences to avoid offending any particular group, they usually disregard cultural differences and identities.

Internationalisation refers to the process of designing a video game in such a way that it can easily be adapted for different languages, cultures, and regions. This includes factors such as ensuring that the game's code is compatible with different character sets and text directions, providing support for different currencies and date formats, and designing user interfaces that are easily understandable by players from different backgrounds. Internationalised video game designing is far more difficult and time-consuming compared to globalised video game design, but it is capable of adapting to various societies and cultures. Internationalisation is important for making a game accessible to a worldwide audience and maximising its potential for success in different markets.

Companies that effectively navigate cultural differences and leverage them to drive innovation and improve their export performance can effectively step toward a successful global marketplace. Goudarz Azar and Rian Drogendijk (2016) verified the relationship between cultural distance, innovation strategy, and export performance, and found that cultural distance can promote managers' innovation decisions and thus improve enterprises' export performance (Lei et al., 2021).

The video games market is expected to grow at an annual rate of 8.76% between 2024 and 2027, resulting in a projected market volume of US$363.20bn by 2027.[1] "Localization can account for 30 to 50% of a publisher's game earnings" (Chandler & Deming, 2011, p. 304). The export of video games beyond their country of origin is a main concern of growing game companies.

> Export entails even larger demand uncertainty and importance of scale economies, because consumer tastes on diverse global export markets are even more unpredictable than at home, and liabilities of foreignness in the guise of diverse stylistic and language preferences are massive.
>
> (Lorenzen, 2007, p. 353)

Exporting video games involves a greater uncertainty compared to other products, as consumer preferences for video games can vary greatly across different cultures and markets.

Adaptation vs. Transformation

Game producers may need to adapt their marketing strategies to each specific market in order to be successful. This can involve customising games and services to better meet the cultural specifications of local consumers. While standardisation may offer some benefits in terms of cost savings and efficiency, companies need to recognise the limitations of this approach and be prepared to be flexible in their marketing strategies to succeed in diverse global markets. This strategy will be practical through either adaptation or transformation.

Adaptation refers to the process of adjusting to new circumstances or environments. Transformation, on the other hand, involves a more radical and fundamental change in form, nature, or character. It often implies a complete restructuring of a game in order to achieve a different outcome. In a video game, adaptation involves making changes to the content and elements of a game to better resonate with the new target culture. This can include translating dialogue, changing character names, altering settings or environments, and adjusting gameplay mechanics to better suit the preferences of players in the new market. By adapting a video game, developers can ensure that cultural references and nuances are accurately portrayed, making the game more relatable and appealing to players in the target culture.

> Supporters of the adaptation of marketing solutions state that, despite the increasing globalization, differences of separate countries when evaluating such dimensions as consumer needs, usage conditions, purchasing power, commercial infrastructure, culture and traditions, laws, and technological development are still very distinct.
>
> (Terpstra & Sarathy, 2000, p. 753)

Transformation involves more comprehensive changes to the structure and design of a video game in order to appeal to the sensibilities and preferences of a new culture. This can include redesigning characters, altering storylines or plot points, reimagining gameplay mechanics, and even changing the overall aesthetics and tone of the game. While transformation may require more effort and resources compared to adaptation, it can result in a more authentic and immersive experience for players in the target culture. By reimagining the game to fit the cultural context and expectations of the new market, developers can create a more compelling and engaging product that resonates with players on a deeper level. It has to be noted that transformation may also risk altering the essence and original vision of the game, potentially alienating or disappointing fans of the original version. Finding the right balance between preserving the core elements of the game and adapting it to the new culture is key to successful transformation.

Legal, Moral, and Religious Issues

Both producing and consuming artistic works always involve various restrictions with regard to legal, moral, and religious concerns. Such concerns can vary greatly between different cultures and countries, due to differing laws, moral norms, and cultural values. Video games today consist of two main components: audiovisual elements, such as images, videos, and sounds and software that manages and allows users to interact with these elements. As a result, some countries classify video games as software assets while others consider them to be artistic works. In countries like Argentina, Canada, China, Italy, or the Russian Federation, jurisprudence or scholars consider video games to be, predominantly, computer programs. A small group of countries, including Kenya and the Republic of Korea, are inclined to think that video games, given their visual elements, are essentially audiovisual works. Countries like Belgium, Brazil, Denmark, Egypt, France, Germany, India, Japan, South Africa, Sweden, and the United States of America, take into account the tremendous complexity of video games in favouring the hypothesis that video games have a distributive classification. As a consequence, legal protection of the different elements of the game must be found separately, according to the specific nature of each work (Ramos et al., 2013, p. 11).

Most often moral norms and religious orders support the laws, but there are cases in which they are not necessarily considered moral or obligatory religious practice. For instance, religious practices in almost all cultures involve the use of sound, such as religious calls, signals, chants, and songs. The right to engage in these practices can sometimes come into conflict with noise regulations or the rights of others to a peaceful environment. In many countries, laws exist to balance the right to religious freedom with the rights of others.

To expand the busyness of video games on an international scale, one has to go through the approach that each country has adopted for the protection of video games and consider the status of the main stakeholders involved in the value chain and in the chain of rights, including authors, publishers, and producers. Lipson and Brain (2009, p. 54) categorise the creative elements of video games as follows:

I. Audio Elements:

   1. Musical Compositions
   2. Sound Recordings
   3. Voice
   4. Imported Sound Effects
   5. Internal Sound Effects

II. Video Elements

   1. Photographic Images
   2. Digitally Captures Moving Images
   3. Animation
   4. Text

III. Computer Code (Source Code and Object Code)

   1. Primary Game Engine or Engines
   2. Ancillary Code
   3. Plug-Ins (Third-Party Subroutines)
   4. Comments

The number of people involved varies depending on the size of the project and the company involved, the kind of video game and the platform for which it was created. Andy Ramos and his colleagues (2013, pp. 9–10) identify these professionals as follows:

Producers:

   i. The Producer (supervisor)
   ii. Production Coordinator
   iii. Assistant Producer
   iv. Associate Producer
   v. Director of Production

b. Game Designers, which include the following:

   i. Lead Designer
   ii. Level Designer
   iii. Content Designer
   iv. Game Writer

v. System Designer
vi. Technical Designer
vii. User Interface Designer
viii. Creative Director
ix. Writer
x. Scriptwriter

c. Artist, the creator of the visual art of the game
d. Programmer or Engineer, who creates and adapts the video game code
e. Audio Designer, responsible for creating sound effects and other related sound elements
f. Owners of neighbouring rights:

i. Performers and Actors, in relation to both voice and movement
ii. Producers of audiovisual and sound recordings

g. Other non-creative positions:

i. Quality Assurance Tester
ii. Publisher of the video game
iii. Accountants
iv. Marketing experts
v. Community Manager

The ownership of copyrights for these professionals will be determined by their level of contribution to the work and the specific laws in each jurisdiction. In general, "in order to be a copyright holder, one must develop original and creative elements or perform the work of another creator such as actors or musicians" (Ramos et al., 2013, p. 10). In many cases, authors have an employer-employee relationship with the company developing the work, resulting in the employer retaining the rights to the work. However, if the work is created outside of this relationship, the producer must ensure the correct transfer of rights in order to properly release and market the video game.

In video games, the producers sometimes benefit from the inherited art of Native people, such as music, images, or/and acts. Such art may be related to ceremonies or assigned to spirituals which are important aspects of the life of indigenous peoples. Legal battles over these issues can become complex, involving questions of religious freedom, cultural preservation, and environmental law. The specifics of these laws can vary greatly among different cultures.

Note

1 www.statista.com

Chapter 1

Geophony and Biophony

The Sound of Nature

Introduction

We are surrounded by nature, and it is the most obvious sensation we have in our life. To bring a sense of reality from a virtual world, the first step is to have a presence of nature to the gamer. Our ears naturally hear all incidents around us, though we do not pay attention to many of them. Consistent surrounding sounds tend to fade into the background for most people. However, if suddenly an absolute silence takes over, it will alert our sensations very quickly and bring our attention back to the missing sounds. Sound helps us to make sense of our social experience and our relation to the community. It also helps us to review how we relate to others, ourselves, and the embodiment of places and spaces.

Although we are surrounded by a variety of natural sounds, we often overlook them as if they don't exist. In an experiment, Bernie Krause (2015, p. 3) participated in a group walk in a California valley, where he recalled hearing vocalisations from four different bird species: a pileated woodpecker, an acorn woodpecker, a ruby-crowned kinglet, and a common raven. He also noted the alarm call of a grey squirrel and the persistent, subtle ambient hush that permeated the valley floor. However, when he asked his fellow walkers the next day to recall any sounds they had heard, only one person remembered the calls of the raven and the pileated woodpecker; none could recall the impact of any other sounds. This lack of attentiveness to nature is a fundamental challenge faced by sound designers in video games. Improving attentive listening to nature is a key strategy to enhance the sound design in video games, particularly to create a dynamic audio landscape.

Think of a humid rainy tropical forest. It is beyond the ability of current gaming devices to simulate the gaming room as hot and humid as you may feel in a real situation, but you can emulate the environmental sound very precisely as if the gamer is really in the forest. In fact, from various identifying ecological aspects of nature in a game, the sound is a sensational element by which we can simulate a place very accurately.

DOI: 10.4324/9781003591399-2

Natural ambient sounds offer a temporal perspective and help define a sense of place. They convey information about the historic era, the time of day, and the changing seasons, revealing that every landscape has its own unique rhythm. For instance, in the south-eastern United States, the vibrant call of the eastern whip-poor-will serves as a nocturnal reminder that warm nights are here. While we, as humans, have grown accustomed to the meanings of these natural sounds, anthropologists have often investigated their rich significance in a holistic cultural context. It is believed that natural and cultural influences on musical experience are in ongoing interaction. In this perspective, nature encompasses all living beings, including humans. Sounds like a baby's cry or bodily noises are natural phenomena; however, when these sounds are repeated and enhanced through technologies such as musical instruments, written notation, and recording devices, they become integrated into cultural practices. Despite their close relationship and moments of merging, nature and culture continue to exist in a state of tension.

Nature Elements

Ancient Persian and Greek scientific traditions classified the components of nature into four primary elements: water (fluidity, adaptability), earth (solidity, stability), fire (heat, energy), and air (lightness, invisibility). Chinese philosophy, particularly Taoism, introduced a slightly different perspective with the five elements theory. This system, known as Wuxing, posits that everything in the universe is interconnected and can be categorised into one of five elements: wood (growth, vitality), fire (passion, transformation), earth (stability, nurture), metal (clarity, precision), and water (wisdom, adaptability). In ancient Indian philosophy, particularly within the context of Ayurveda, the classical elements are described as five in number: earth, water, fire, air, and ether. "Ether" or *akasha* serves as a foundational tenet in Indian metaphysical thought, which highlights the interconnectivity of the physical and spiritual worlds.[1] These ancient elemental theories, while differing in their specific details, share a common objective: to comprehend the fundamental nature of the universe and humanity's place within it. They offer valuable insights into the human mind's pursuit of understanding the world around us.

To decide what background sounds we should include in the soundtrack to give a natural sensation to gamers we can consider the nature elements. We have some key questions to answer:

- How far is the location of the scene from the sea?
- How rainy, dry, or humid is the climate?
- What is the situation of the forecast at the dramatic time of the game?
- Does the story of the game take place on planet Earth; if not, what is the weather on that planet look like?
- What is the topography of the location of the scene?
- What is the elevation of the land from the sea?

- What is the situation of the sun – and other stars – in the sky?
- How shiny is the sky?
- In what season does the story of the game take place?
- What is the speed and direction of the wind?
- Is the weather smooth or stormy?
- Do the game characters depend on oxygen, water, or any other thing to stay alive?

An artist may inspire his/her imagination of the possible environmental natural sound by trying to answer the above questions, even if the location in the game exists nowhere in the world. Let us consider a hypothetical game scene that takes place in a fantasy world, where we can draw on the elements outlined in the above questions. The scene unfolds in a dense, enchanted forest located far from any sea, on the planet *Armaiti*. The forest is shrouded in an early morning mist, hinting at a mysterious atmosphere.

1. How far is the location of the scene from the sea?
   - Details: The enchanted forest is several hundred miles inland.
   - Sound Consideration: The soundtrack will not contain any ocean sounds but will focus on forest ambiance, such as rustling leaves and distant animal calls.
2. How rainy, dry, or humid is the climate?
   - Details: The climate is humid, with frequent light rains and mist.
   - Sound Consideration: Include subtle sounds of dripping water, soft rain patter, and intermittent squelching of wet ground underfoot.
3. What is the situation of the forecast at the dramatic time of the game?
   - Details: It is a calm morning with a chance of rain later in the day.
   - Sound Consideration: Begin with soft rain sounds, marking the calm before a potential storm.
4. Does the story of the game take place on planet Earth; if not what is the weather on that planet look like?
   - Details: The game takes place on planet *Armaiti* (in a fantasy world), which has similar flora but unique magical properties that occasionally affect weather patterns.
   - Sound Consideration: Introduce sounds of mythical creatures – for instance, the distant call of a faerie or the flutter of magical wings.
5. What is the topography of the location of the scene?
   - Details: The forest is lush with rolling hills and thick undergrowth.
   - Sound Consideration: Background sounds include the rustling of bushes and trees swaying gently in response to breezes.

6. What is the elevation of the land from the sea?
   - Details: The forest is about 500 feet above sea level, atop a low hill.
   - Sound Consideration: Gentle wind sounds to indicate higher elevation, creating an ethereal feel.
7. What is the situation of the sun – and other stars – in the sky?
   - Details: The sun is just rising, casting a warm golden light through the trees.
   - Sound Consideration: Harmonious, uplifting ambient sounds to evoke the feeling of a new day.
8. How shiny is the sky?
   - Details: The sky is mostly clear with a few clouds, allowing sunlight to come through.
   - Sound Consideration: A soft breeze sound, with a light to reflect the cheerful atmosphere.
9. In what season does the story of the game take place?
   - Details: It is early spring, with flowers beginning to bloom.
   - Sound Consideration: The inclusion of bird songs and the sound of buzzing insects to emphasise the liveliness of spring.
10. What is the speed and direction of the wind?
    - Details: A light breeze coming from the east.
    - Sound Consideration: Gentle wind sounds that indicate the breeze, with occasional whispers of the trees moving.
11. Is the weather smooth or stormy?
    - Details: The weather is currently smooth, but a storm is forecast later in the afternoon.
    - Sound Consideration: Create foreboding undertones but maintain a calm overall ambiance.
12. Do the game characters depend on oxygen, water, or any other thing to stay alive?
    - Details: Yes, the characters depend on oxygen and water from the forest ecosystem.
    - Sound Consideration: A lively water sound from a nearby stream occasionally is heard to indicate a vital water source.

The resulting soundtrack would seamlessly blend these natural sounds to create a rich, immersive experience that captures the enchanting, serene atmosphere of the scene. At the same time, it subtly hints at the potential for dramatic change as the game gradually unfolds.

Climate

Many factors influence both the weather and the overall climate of a location, which we need to consider when creating our visual and audio elements in game design. The most important of these factors include warmth, air pressure, air movement, sunlight, moisture, rain or snow, changes in state, and the lay of the land. These elements plus human roles as both individual and social modulators, animals (zoogeography), and plants (phytogeography) shape the environmental characteristics of every spot on Earth (and other planets).

One can make a table of various natural sounds typical to every climate, such as rainforest, desert, Arctic, coastal, green mountain, frozen mountain, and so on. However, the problem with such generalisation is disregarding the cultural identity of the landscape. Different regions and cultures may have unique sounds that are specific to their particular climate and environment. For example, the sound of waves crashing on a beach is influenced by several factors, resulting in the auditory experiences of gamers. The nature of the waves – whether they are gentle swells or fierce, choppy surf – plays a crucial role, as does the contour of the coastline and the underlying geological features of the area. A tranquil beach might feature soft, rolling waves that create a soothing lullaby, while a rugged coastline may host powerful tidal waves or even destructive tsunamis. The composition of the beach itself – sandy expanses versus rocky outcroppings – further alters the sound, as does the temperature of the water, ranging from warm tropical currents to the chilling embrace of northern seas. Moreover, the ambiance of urban beaches, often accompanied by the hum of city life, contrasts sharply with the serene, untouched sounds of remote beaches, where nature reigns supreme and the only sound is the gentle caress of waves against the beach.

The number of climate IDs that we can represent by sound is very limited. Moreover, we cannot show factors such as solar irradiance or atmospheric pressure directly through sound effects. There are some typical sound effects for a certain climate that may come to mind for every sound designer to illustrate the feeling of being at the seaside, tropical rainforest, mountain forest, and so on. Nonetheless, the reason why we intentionally concentrate on specific ambient sounds while disregarding others is influenced by various factors, with cultural influences standing out as a key component. Imagine two distinct coastal cultures with similar climates. In one, the sea is a vital food source and is deeply revered in the local customs. In the other, residents work mainly in factories and view the sea primarily as a scenic natural feature. Think what the central attention in the sound effect of a stormy night will be in each of the above cultures.

Whereas people in San Francisco live on the coastline with little or no daily relation to the sea, the Moken people of Thailand and Myanmar have an interlocked relationship with the sea.

> They are all strand-dwellers living either on boats or on the beach. The main exception to this seems to be some of the Moklen whose settlements are a kilometre or more from the sea. Their whole culture is based on the gathering of sea produce, tripang, shellfish, fish, lobsters, coral and shells of different types.
>
> (Hogan, 1972, p. 213)

The Moken rely on the sea for their food, livelihoods, and cultural identity. They are skilled fishermen and free divers, harvesting a variety of seafood, such as fish, shellfish, and sea cucumbers. They also gather sea cucumbers, seaweed, and other marine resources for trade and barter. In Moken culture, the sea is revered as a source of life and sustenance. They believe that the sea is a spiritual entity that provides for them and protects them. The Moken language contains many words related to the sea and marine life, reflecting their close connection to the ocean. They also have traditional songs, dances, and rituals that celebrate the sea and honour the spirits of the water.

The example above illustrates how the emphasis on the soundscape of the sea can vary in mixing audio tracks, depending on the location. A beach in Thailand may evoke a different auditory experience compared to a beach in San Francisco, influenced by the distinct cultural contexts of the people in these two regions.

People in the forest believe that noise kills the forest. There is a strong belief in appreciation of the sound of nature among tribes such as the Pygmy people. Forest from the view of the Pygmy looks like God, honourable and fearful despite the food provider and nutrition of the man. Their songs somehow imitate the natural sound of birds and other animals and creatures of the forests. It shows how nature's sound may integrate with culture and the way people live.

Biophony: Animals and Species

The sound of birds chirping may be associated with forests or jungles in general, but the specific species of birds and their unique calls can vary significantly depending on the geographical location. In some cases, certain bird species may even be endemic to a particular region, making their sounds an integral part of the cultural identity of that area.

In a broad classification, I categorise animals and creatures on the scene into four different types:

- Animal and species that are already living on Earth and we have experienced their voices or sounds
- Those who are already living on Earth but make no audible voice or sound such as ants and spiders

- The extinct animals or creatures
- Imaginary and sci-fi creatures such as tribbles and semi-human semi-animals such as the centaur

In the enchanting realms of animation and video games, various species and creatures often communicate in human language, or they speak in their own distinct manner. However, players can easily follow the conversation through dialogue boxes that display captions of their exchanges. In some cases, they have a non-verbal voice, and the audience needs to guess what they say as they are trying to make a semantic communication. In both cases, large characters typically have a low frequency and tiny or small characters have high-frequency voices. There is also the possibility that they make sounds other than their conventional or natural sounds, for instance *Road Runner* sounds beep beep and makes a sound like a racing car. Whatever the sound strategy of the director is, we cannot keep the animal characters soundless in an animation or video game except for those who have no dramatic role and stay in the background.

Now, the question is how animal sounds can be in track with cultural identity. Animal sounds can evoke a variety of meanings and emotions that are deeply intertwined with cultural beliefs, practices, and values. For instance, the distinction between the voices of Asian and African elephants not only reflects the biological differences between these species but also aligns with the cultural significance each holds in different societies. In some cultures, elephants may symbolise wisdom and strength, while in others, they may represent labour and utility. This cultural framing influences how people perceive these animals and their vocalisations, which can range from gentle rumbles to trumpet calls, each carrying its own cultural connotations.

Similarly, the treatment of animals in different cultures highlights divergent attitudes toward nature and life. In Spain, the tradition of bullfighting is steeped in history and is often viewed as a form of art or spectacle, despite its controversial nature. The sounds associated with this event – the roaring of the crowd, the snorts of the bull, and the music played – create a charged atmosphere that reflects the cultural significance placed on machismo and bravery.

In contrast, Hindu culture's reverence for cows as symbols of life and non-violence emphasises a different set of values. The cow's gentle mooing and the serene sounds of pastoral life contrast sharply with the dramatic, tension-filled environment of a bullfight. The principle of *ahimsa*, which advocates for the non-harm of all living beings, informs how many Hindus perceive and respond to animal sounds, urging a more compassionate relationship with the animal world.

These cultural distinctions are not only reflected in the ways animals are treated but also in the soundscapes that accompany those interactions. In the case of bullfighting, music and cheers can enhance the drama, while in Hindu contexts, chants and devotional sounds might accompany rituals honouring cows.

Precautions have to be taken about the audience, too. In situations like the above example, we cannot simply expect a cartoon produced based on the cultural norm of Western Europe to be treated as normal by the people of South Asia.

To what extent can the sounds and voices of an animal deliver his/her characteristics in a video game or animation? Well, it directly depends on how much visual and dramatic parts play a role in shaping the character of an animal and what remains for the soundtrack to fill. If we are facing a simplified and hyper-casual genre in which there is very little place for visualisation of the characters on the scene, we will expect a great deal to be filled by the other media, such as the storyline and the soundtrack. On the other hand, if we benefit from verbal communication by an animal or creature in a movie or game, we will be able to put a huge part of character formation on the soundtrack, but if the strategy of the director is to use non-verbal voices or sounds, we may expect rather less from sound to shape the characteristics for every individual animal on the scene.

The emotions and moods of an animal character are another important matter in animations and games. Pythagoreans consider various emotional senses of animals. They also believe that there are shared grounds between human and animal experiences of emotions (Coates, 1998). Researches provide experimental evidence that at least some animals likely feel a full range of emotions, including fear, joy, happiness, shame, embarrassment, resentment, jealousy, rage, anger, love, pleasure, compassion, respect, relief, disgust, sadness, despair, and grief (Bekoff, 2000). Scientists also seek to decode the emotional sounds of animals. In 2022 scientists from the University of Copenhagen published an article stating they can now decode pigs' emotions based on an algorithm they found in their experimental research:

> Using more than 7000 audio recordings of pigs, the researchers designed an algorithm that can decode whether an individual pig is experiencing a positive emotion ("happy" or "excited"), a negative one ("scared" or "stressed"), or somewhere in between. The recordings were collected in a wide range of situations encountered by commercial pigs, both positive and negative, from when they are born until their deaths. With this study, we demonstrate that animal sounds provide great insight into their emotions.
>
> (Briefer et al., 2022)

Different moods of animals will be perceived mostly by their owners, who have spent years communicating, and it is hard to describe such moods in various circumstances by the owners verbally. When a dog is taken to an animal practitioner or veterinarian, the owner tries to use the senses he/she perceives from his/her animal to describe the problem. Such symptoms may not be directly apparent to the practitioner in an ordinary examination. What I mean by that is that to illustrate the various audiovisual moods of animals, one has to live with animals.

Cartoonists typically adapt human emotional behaviours to draw their characters in different moods. In cases where a character talks like a human, the sound artist uses human emotional verbal and non-verbal voices to deliver the right emotion through the dialogue tracks, too. However, in situations where an animal character does not talk in human language, we need to build the soundtrack in a more artistic way. Here is the place where culture steps forward again. People of one culture may believe a certain sound of a wolf shows anger, while the same sound may be considered sorrowful in a different culture. Nevertheless, it is crucial to recognise that biophony and geophony aspects are not static elements within an environment. Rather, they are dynamic and subject to constant change. Factors such as species migration, fluctuating populations, and environmental shifts like desertification can drastically alter the acoustic landscape over time. Hence, we need to collect a catalogue of animal sounds and voices and seek to find the right one for every emotion from the point of view of people of that culture. The answers to our inquiry may not always give a hundred percent agreement from all members of the society, but we can get the idea of the majority about emotions delivered by every local animal sound.

Watch emotional scenes of Dumbo by Tim Burton (2019) and pay attention to the voices of Dumbo in different scenes, including when they dress him up in clown makeup and force him to humiliate himself in front of the crowds also when he visits his mother after she's been locked in a carriage. The problem, however, is that like most other Hollywood products, you hear a "universal" tone rather than a specific culture.

In Peruvian movies, you can often notice several cultural features portrayed in both the visual and audio components. For example, in a documentary photo taken by Katherine Needles featuring a Peruvian tribal boy with his hunting arrow, you can observe elements that showcase the indigenous culture of Peru. These visual cues provide a glimpse into their way of life and beliefs (Compare the documentary photo of a Peruvian tribal boy with his hunting arrow taken by Katherine Needles with a scene of the Peruvian animation *Ainbo: Spirit of the Amazon* in Figure 1.1).

The same will be seen in Iranian or Armenian movies. However, when a Peruvian film director gets a job in Hollywood, you can hardly trace any sounds and images indicating his cultural background in his or her films. In fact, directors try to create films that belong to nowhere in particular, prioritising themes and storytelling styles that transcend any specific cultural context. This often entails diluting or even erasing the specific cultural elements that may limit the film's appeal or accessibility outside of its country of origin. Many non-Western filmmakers have faced similar challenges when

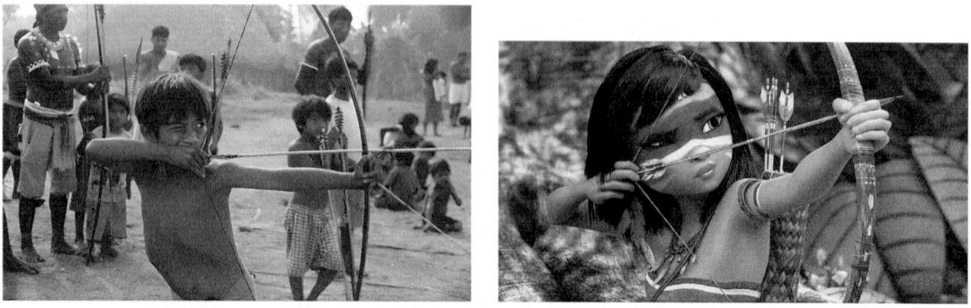

Figure 1.1 When you step out of Hollywood, you can get more sense of cultures in movies and animations. Compare tribal hunting boy with heroine character of animation *Ainbo: Spirit of the Amazon* (left: photo by Paula Mendonça originally contributed to the civil society organisation of ISA in in São Paulo, right: screen capture from *Ainbo: Spirit of the Amazon* directed by Richard Claus and Jose Zelada)

trying to break into the global film industry. This phenomenon has led to debates about cultural representation, authenticity, and the impact of cultural homogenisation in cinema.

An artistical-anthropological approach I offer to make a soundtrack based on cultural norms but dynamic enough to use in various dramatic circumstances in different scenes of the game is to provide a good collection of animal voices samples from the field where the story takes place and analyse their spectrum to find the main sound specifications, including contour, harmonic, timbre, and other structural elements. The recording must meet the standards of ethnography field recording which means taking note of local people's beliefs and interpretations about every recorded sound in the field. Here is what Stanisz (2017, p. 1) says about the recording in the field:

> Field recording must be understood as one of the research methods of sonic ethnography and a way to create alternative representations of fieldwork knowledge. Application of field recording in ethnographic research makes it possible to track down social patterns, connections between collective emotions, auditory practices and social structures, which usually remain hidden and faded out in textual representations. Doing field recordings also allows the researcher to experience anthropological fieldwork in a more sensuous and immersive way.

Once you have incorporated all the relevant structural and anthropological components, you can make adjustments to ensure that the sound complements each scene, while still appealing to the preferences of the inhabited audience. For example, in central Africa, social rumbling can be heard among elephants when one of their group members passes away, leading to audible

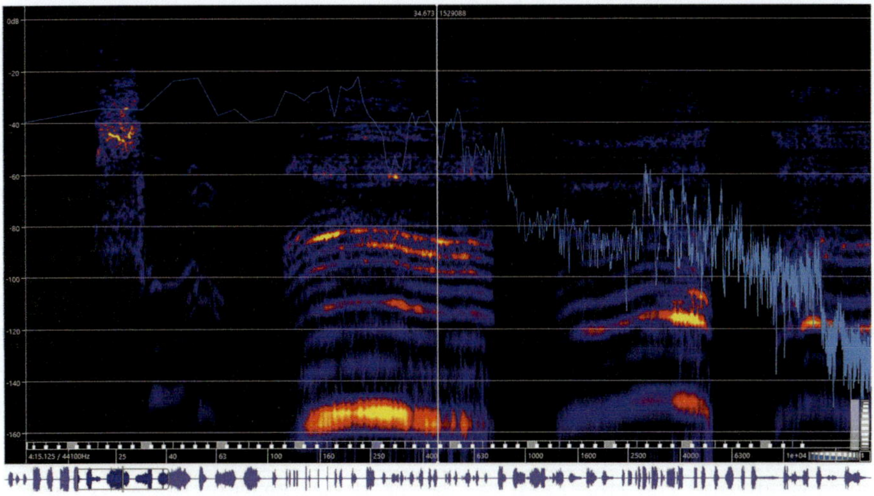

Figure 1.2 Spectrum analysis of African elephant trumpeting (Sonic Visualiser App, photo by author)

sounds of agitation. The African elephant's roaring entirely differs from his rumbling. The rumbling is like a human talking. Baby elephants make a begging rumble so they can suckle milk. When males are searching for a mate, they emit a pulsating musth rumble. Females respond with their own estrous rumbles, making them as loud as possible so they can alert more males. There are many different rumbles used for greetings and to persuade the herd to do something. Elephant trumpeting is like human shouting. The following figure is a spectrum analysis of an African Elephant trumpeting in his excitement.

Strategies for Creating Voices for Inaudible Creatures

Designing voice or sound effects for creatures that do not produce audible sounds in reality, like ants and spiders, requires some creativity. Before we start our creative part, we need to study the behaviour and movements of the creature. We also need to closely observe the creature's actions in various situations and circumstances. It helps to identify analogous sounds. Analogous sounds can evoke a similar feeling or essence to the creature we are working on.

One approach is to employ specialised sound recording devices capable of capturing sounds that are typically inaudible to the human ear, such as those produced by insects or marine creatures. These recordings can be amplified and transformed into frequencies that humans can hear. Subsequently, artistic enhancements can be applied to the sound, making it more compelling and suitable for incorporation into audio tracks.

Spatialisation is another technique to match a sound to a creature's characteristics. By placing the sounds in different locations within the stereo or surround sound field, you can create a sense of movement or proximity based on the creature's actions.

If we did not find any analogous sound in nature, we may think of Foley techniques. Foley is the art of creating sound effects by manipulating physical objects or digital audio workstations (DAWs). In this technique, we experiment with various materials and objects to achieve the desired sounds. We can make a combination sound of physical objects with the Fx of DAWs. It helps to adjust the pitch, speed, and intensity of the sounds to make them unobtrusive and subtle. We have to be patient. We need to play around with different combinations of sounds, layers, and effects until it feels organic and authentic to the creature's behaviour.

Regardless of approach, when designing voice or sound effects for creatures that do not produce audible sounds, it is essential to consider cultural perceptions and the emotional resonance these creatures have in various societies. For instance in several cultures including Western society, ants are often seen as industrious, social, or even militaristic creatures; ants can be attributed to voices that are collaborative, harmonious, or even authoritative. Drawing on imagery such as hive minds or teamwork could inspire a collective humming or rhythmic patterns representing their industrious nature. Similarly, in Japanese culture, ants are admired for their teamwork and diligence. However, in some African traditions, ants are viewed as guides or messengers, carrying meanings related to perseverance. Creating voices for unvoiced creatures challenges the bounds of sound design and calls for a melding of cultural context with imaginative audio representation.

Strategies for Creating Voices for Extinct Animals or Creatures

The first step for creating voices for extinct animals is studying reliable sources to gather as much information as possible about their appearance, behaviour, habitat, and biological characteristics. We can seek assistance from palaeontologists, biologists, or other experts in the field who specialise in extinct animals or creatures. They can help to provide information about the shape of the larynx and other organs by which the animal or species used to make sound signals.

The other thing that we may find useful is identifying modern-day animals or creatures that share similarities with the extinct animal we are trying to create a voice for. Analysing the vocalisations, body language, and other communication methods used by these related species can offer valuable insights into how the extinct animal may have communicated. The nature of animals' environment provides valuable information about how they possibly communicate. Animals adapt their sounds to suit their environment, so understanding the context in which the extinct animals live can help us create a more realistic voice for them.

While scientific accuracy is important, it is also crucial to use creativity and artistic interpretation to fill in the gaps in knowledge. We can combine the available historical and scientific findings with our imagination to create a unique and acceptable voice. To pursue this goal, we may collaborate with artists, writers, sound designers, and other creative professionals to improve our creativity.

Despite, palaeontology and bioacoustics have developed methods to recreate what extinct animal voices may have sounded like, the cultural perspective toward them can vary across different societies and contexts. Many cultures have myths, stories, or songs that reference extinct animals, viewing them as significant to their historical narratives or spiritual beliefs. For example, the woolly mammoth or the dodo bird may feature in legends that reflect a society's relationship with nature and awareness of extinction. Different cultures may have particular reverence for extinct species, viewing them as symbols of change and continuity within ecosystems and emphasising the lessons learned from their disappearance.

Strategies for Creating Voices for Imaginary and Sci-Fi Creatures

People from different social backgrounds may perceive imaginary and science fiction creatures in video games differently due to their cultural beliefs, mythologies, social norms, and historical contexts. Many cultures have their own mythological creatures that can influence how they view similar beings in video games. For example, a dragon in Western cultures is often depicted as a fearsome beast, whereas in some Asian cultures, dragons can symbolise wisdom and benevolence. This can lead to different emotional responses and engagements with dragon-like creatures in games. Moreover, creatures that embody specific personalities may resonate differently across cultures. For instance, a creature that symbolises strength might be perceived positively in some cultures while being viewed sceptically in others. For example, predatory animals may evoke fear in cultures that value harmony and pastoral living, while being revered in cultures with warrior traditions.

Another issue that may influence the way people of different societies perceive imaginary characters differently is the aesthetic norms and philosophy. Characters with exaggerated features might be seen as cute and endearing in one culture but could be viewed as grotesque in another. The overall art style (e.g., cartoonish vs. realistic) can also influence perceptions. The backstory and role of the creature within the game's narrative can also affect perception. A creature that plays a villain in a game may resonate differently with players from cultures that have different views on heroism and villainy. It is also true in the theme that a game designer chooses for the game. In some cultures, certain themes associated with certain creatures – such as death, resurrection, or technology's impact on nature – may be more sensitive or taboo, influencing how those creatures are received in gameplay. A creature that symbolises technological advancement might be embraced in cultures that prioritise innovation, while in cultures with a history of colonialism or technological disruption, the same creature might be viewed with suspicion or scepticism.

Creating a unique, compelling voice for imaginary and sci-fi creatures can greatly enhance their believability and impact in video games. Most often both the appearance and voice of characters in sci-fi are created simultaneously. In some cases, particularly for pre-existing works adapted into sci-fi video game characters, the appearance and voice of the character may be determined prior to the adaptation. For example, if a sci-fi character is based on a comic book or novel, the appearance and characteristics of the character may have already been established in the source material. In such cases, the visual design and voice may need to align with the established portrayal in order to stay true to the original intention within that culture.

Note

1 There is a fifth element in Japanese philosophy called void or *ku*. The concept of void represents the essence or potential of existence.

Chapter 2

Anthropophony

Soundscape and Sonic Ethnology

Introduction

For environmental activists, the manmade sounds may bring negative consequences of noise pollution in mind, particularly for ecology and zoology scientists who have spent years studying how human noises are interfering with animal communication, hindering their foraging abilities, and impacting where they live. In this book, however, the manmade sound is an initial part of human culture and ritual on Earth which not only is not a bad thing but also gives meaning to our social life. Our lives on Earth make various noises which sometimes are in accordance and sometimes are against sounds of nature. In this chapter, we explore the ways in which sound and acoustics shape and influence human experiences, behaviours, and identities in cities and villages. We seek to understand how people perceive, interpret, and interact with their sonic environment, as well as the meanings and significance they attribute to different sounds. This field of study emerged from the broader field of soundscape studies, which was pioneered by Canadian composer R. Murray Schafer in the 1970s.

In this chapter, I am particularly interested in the relational and experiential aspects of sound that cut across dichotomies between nature and culture, non-musical sound and music, or as Feld (1996) signifies relationships of sound, species, places, and meanings. I examine sound as a crucial aspect of life as Walter Ong (1967, p. 112) suggests "Sound must be in active production in order to exist at all."

Music, sound effects, and dialogue are the traditional pillars of video game audio. However, the cultural context of gamers often challenges this conventional categorisation. The dynamic interplay of audio elements shapes not only the gaming experience but also influences broader trends in music, visual means, and digital communication. The active role of gamers in shaping the audio experience, combined with ever-evolving technology, has resulted in unique sonic landscapes. This interaction between categories not only enhances immersion but also highlights the cultural significance of gamers as co-creators of the audio experience.

DOI: 10.4324/9781003591399-3

Combining the study of sound and music with ethnographic research makes the basis of "sonic ethnology" or "sound ethnography." It involves exploring the role of sound in culture, social life, and identity formation of people. The social, economical, industrial, and eventually cultural changes greatly reflect on the soundscape of a city, town, or village. Our surrounding environment is full of various sounds which influence our emotions, thoughts, and behaviours. By analysing the soundscape of a particular place or community, researchers can gain a deeper understanding of the meanings and values that are attached to different sounds and music.

Stokes made a statement about how "[a] sense of identity can be put into place through music by performing it, dancing to it, listening to it or even thinking about it" (1994, p. 24). I assume observation of Stokes is capable of being applied to sonic environments, though musical performances may be only one element out of several sonic elements. In an environmental context, the soundscape helps us understand the acoustical culture and ecology of a place. Field study of soundscape benefits in two different ways, which are not necessarily in opposition: to deepen the relationship between the production of sound and its environment, and to concentrate on an aural ethnography that investigates the ways sound is perceived and treated by the members of the society. A Middle East bazaar is filled with the sound of handicraft makers, arguing of shopkeepers trading with customers, singing of wondering sellers, belling from a nearby church, reciting the call to prayer of muezzins atop the minarets of mosques, and many other sounds heard one after the other or simultaneously. Paying attention to the surrounding sounds is crucial for providing information about the world around us. I call it the "sonic ethnology" of home town. This notion allows us to figure out how residents communally sense, recognise, experience, and respond to the sound of their living place. "Sound, in this perspective, becomes a tool to mark ritual space and organise action and serve as a marker of local identities" (Ferrarini & Scaldaferri, 2020, p. 3). In this regard we can call this concept "soundmark" as Schafer (1977) suggests.

Michiel Kamp (2021, p. 168) posits a thought-provoking question: why would someone seek out another person's description of playing a video game with music when they can experience it firsthand? He argues that autoethnography can offer valuable insights into the subjective nature of sound perception and the ways in which cultural context enriches the overall video game experience.

The answer lies in the unique lens through which each individual perceives and interprets their surroundings. Cultural context, shaped by factors such as upbringing, life experiences, and physiological differences, provides a distinctive framework for understanding and appreciating soundscapes. By exploring these cultural nuances, autoethnography can offer a deeper understanding of how video game audio is experienced and interpreted across diverse populations.

This perspective is echoed in the realm of video game music, where radio stations often serve as a direct connection to the real world. As Miller suggests, radio music can emphasise the authentic soundscape of a society. She argues in her ethnographic study of *San Andreas*, "The only direct product placement in the games is the music on the radio, a design choice that creates a powerful musical connection between the gameworlds and the real world" (Miller, 2012, p. 54).

The heterogeneity of a landscape is another issue which enters the study of sound into a challenging phase. Almo Farina and his colleagues (2014) stress the heterogeneity of the Mediterranean landscapes, as their inhabitants are also heterogeneous. During the day, one might hear the *adhan* call to prayer, the sound of the church bell, and other religion-related sounds, such as the liturgy, a prayer, or the sound of the people who gather on the occasion of a ceremony.

> A soundscape with a fine spatial and temporal resolution, and a result of this parallel behaviour of sounds to landscape structure, soundscape indices (such as acoustic complexity or diversity) will be important indicators for ecosystem dynamics across human-dominated, complex landscapes.
>
> (Farina et al., 2014, p. 11)

Sonic Ethnology of Industrial Workstations

The soundscape of industrial workplaces is a reflection of the social, cultural, and historical contexts of industrial labour. It illuminates how workers interact with their environment and with each other. The use of machinery and tools, and the social interactions among workers give insight into the rhythms of the life of workers. The music and other media played at a workplace as a way to pass the time or to stay motivated gives us a taste of life in a workstation. We can explore the role that music and other forms of sound play in shaping the experiences and identities of industrial workers. Here is a case, the Great Britain industry soundscape prior to World War II (See Parry & Lane, 2005).

Singing in factories has long been recognised as a form of resistance and resilience among workers facing harsh and noisy working conditions. It can foster a sense of community among workers, creating bonds that help them cope with their challenging environment. Nearly all workers of any individual factory know the songs popular in their workplace, which reinforces unity and collective identity. Workers often experience a range of emotions, from frustration to joy. Singing allows workers to express their individual and collective feelings about their circumstances, whether those feelings are of hardship, defiance, or hope. In many cases, workers have used songs to create a rhythm that aligns with their work tasks. This can enhance productivity by providing a steady tempo that helps maintain a consistent and efficient pace. Singing often incorporates folk traditions and cultural expressions, allowing

Table 2.1 Great Britain industry soundscape prior to World War II

Soundscape sources	*Soundscape effects*
Factory Machinery	The sounds of various machines and equipment that could include the rhythmic clanking of metal presses, the whirring of spinning machines in textile mills, the hiss of steam engines, the buzzing of electric motors, and the clattering of conveyor belts.
Steam Engines	Steam power in mining, manufacturing, and transportation that would have included the chugging of steam engines, the release of steam from valves, the hissing of pressure being released, and the occasional whistle or horn signalling shifts or breaks.
Hammering and Metalworking	Industries like blacksmithing, iron foundries, and shipbuilding would have featured the sounds of hammering, pounding, and shaping metal. The rhythmic beats of hammers on anvils, the clang of metal being struck, and the metallic resonance of large-scale forging would have contributed to the soundscape.
Tools and Handcrafting	Craftsmen and artisans working with wood, leather, and other materials would have produced their own unique sounds. This could include the scraping of chisels, the sawing of wood, the tapping of hammers, and the sound of hand-operated tools being used for shaping, carving, or polishing materials.
Steam Whistles and Signals	Steam whistles were commonly used to signal the start and end of shifts, breaks, and other important events. These loud, shrill whistles would have been audible from a distance, cutting through the overall soundscape of the surrounding area.
Transportation	The transportation-related sounds could include the clatter of horse-drawn carts on cobblestone streets, the rumble of early motor vehicles, the screeching of railway wheels, and the occasional blast of a ship's horn in port areas.

workers to preserve their heritage and share their stories, values, and struggles through music. This cultural continuity can be empowering in challenging environments.

Amadeu Corbera Jaume and Eulàlia Febrer Coll (2019) reviewed the costume jewellery workers' and shoemakers' experience of Menorca in the Balearic Islands, to show the processes of resistance and resilience in the transition from a pre-industrial culture to capitalism. Here is part of the workers' interviews report by Jaume and Coll (2019, p. 11):

> Then, because the radio was kind of boring, we bought a lot of records. . . . Whoever was closer [to the machine] put the records on, or maybe someone was walking by and that recording had ended so they changed it.
>
> (Eulàlia Serra Truyol, Ferreries)

> The record collection that we had here was impressive. . . . There was people that maybe didn't like sarsuela, and "well, we could play some other kind of music, this is so boring, every day . . ." Usually, it was the manager who was in charge, and sometime after it was someone else.
>
> (Juan Fernando Palliser Sintes, Alaior)

> Music was there when factories opened in cellars, then they sang. . . . Afterwards, when working with an assembly line one had to shut up. . . . With an assembly line you can't work . . . and sing.
>
> (Toni Riudavets Salom, Ferreries)

The cultural meanings and values attached to industrial work. Industrial sounds can serve as a powerful narrative device in games, shaping the player's perception of the game world and its inhabitants. For example, the soundscape of a factory may be associated with ideas of productivity, efficiency, and progress, or with ideas of monotony, alienation, and exploitation.

Setting the tone for audio tracks in stories that take place in industrial sites involves various factors. For instance, harsh, metallic sounds and repetitive mechanical sounds can create a sense of oppression and dehumanisation, while warmer sounds like steam whistles and factory bells can evoke feelings of nostalgia and longing. Industrial sound effects can also be used to develop characters in games. For example, the sounds of heavy machinery and repetitive tasks can highlight the physical and emotional toll of labour.

Sonic Ethnology of Busyness, Sports, and Entertainment

In this section, I explore how sound and music intersect with the sonic ethnology of busyness, sports, and entertainment which may play a significant role in cultural identity. The sonic identities of European cities have been extensively discussed by Amphoux (1993). He highlighted that in sonic, spatial, and sociocultural dimensions, the listeners' impressions of the surrounding sounds can provide a satisfying description of the urban sonic identity of a place. The soundscape of busyness, sports, and entertainment are event-related phenomena which influence each other in various ways and promote a sense of collective social experiences.

Busyness

In the context of busyness, sound plays a crucial role in shaping our perception and experience of productivity, efficiency, and the fast-paced nature of modern life. The transition from farm life to busyness life relocated people from nature to urban. "A relocation of people would necessarily include the relocation and change of the resonance of their everyday activities" (Christidis & Quinton, 2016, p. 104).

A close examination of the soundscapes of different states reveals that the soundscape of busyness is not monolithic; instead, it varies significantly across different cultural contexts. For example, the auditory landscape of African marketplaces is a vibrant acoustic woven from polyrhythmic drumming, the enthusiastic calls of vendors, and the joyful harmonies of communal singing and dancing. In contrast, countries like Japan showcase unique auditory experiences, where the energy of everyday life is captured in the bustling atmospheres of street markets and entrepreneurial activities.

The opportunity to explore and incorporate the soundscapes of busyness from various cultures significantly enriches the auditory dimension of video game design. By blending the distinctive sounds from different cultural settings, designers can forge an immersive auditory experience that not only mirrors the frenetic pace of contemporary life but also honours the richness and diversity of global cultures. This intentional curation of sound transcends mere background sound, transforming everyday auditory markers into an engaging and educational element that enhances players' appreciation for the cultural heritage of the world around them.

Sports

Sound and music have a significant impact on the world of sports, both for the athletes and the spectators. In sports events, music is often used to create an energetic and engaging atmosphere. Stadium anthems, team chants, and victory songs are examples of how music becomes intertwined with the emotional experience of sports. Additionally, sound effects, such as buzzers, whistles, and crowd reactions, enhance the overall excitement and drama of the game. In some cases, specific songs or genres of music become associated with certain sports, teams, or athletes, creating a sonic identity and a sense of unity among fans.

Sonic elements play a significant role in embodying a culture's sporting traditions, profoundly influencing the collective identity of communities. In Latin American countries, sports like soccer (football) are deeply ingrained in everyday life, and this is reflected in their vibrant soundscapes. The lively crowd chants, rhythmic drumming, and energetic brass instruments create an immersive sonic atmosphere that resonates with the passion and exuberance for the sport in the region. For example, the distinctive beats of samba music in Brazil are intertwined with the country's soccer culture, reinforcing its cultural identity.

In the context of video game audio, these sonic traditions can be harnessed to enhance the gaming experience. By incorporating authentic crowd sounds, traditional musical elements, and dynamic soundscapes, game developers can create an immersive environment that reflects the cultural significance of sports like soccer. Imagine a soccer video game featuring real-time crowd reactions, samba-infused background music, and dynamic audio cues that capture the excitement of a match. Such elements not only enrich gameplay but also connect players to the cultural roots of the sport.

Similarly, in countries like Japan and South Korea, traditional martial arts such as sumo, judo, and taekwondo are characterised by rich soundscapes that include ceremonial rituals, drumming, and the vocal expressions of practitioners. In a video game centred around martial arts, these sonic elements can be integrated to evoke the discipline, respect for tradition, and physical prowess associated with these sports, thereby deepening the player's engagement with the cultural context.

Here I provide a case of the soundscape of a traditional sport in Afghanistan called *Buzkashi* (goat grabbing). The traditional sport of Buzkashi in Afghanistan has a distinct and vibrant soundscape that adds to the overall experience and cultural significance of the game. *Buzkashi* is a traditional equestrian sport played mainly in central Asian countries, including Afghanistan (Azoy, 1982). The soundscape combines the natural sounds of horses, the vocal expressions of the players, the traditional music, and the reactions of the crowd, creating a multisensory experience that immerses participants and observers alike in the rich cultural heritage of Afghanistan:

- **Hooves and Galloping:** The thundering sound of horses' hooves is an integral part of the *Buzkashi* soundscape (Azoy, 1982, p. 56). As the players chase after the carcass of a goat or calf, the rhythmic galloping of the horses creates a powerful and intense auditory experience.
- **Shouts and Calls:** The players, known as Chapandaz, often shout and call out to each other during the game. These vocalisations serve multiple purposes, such as coordinating strategies, expressing excitement, and intimidating opponents. The shouts and calls blend with the sounds of the horses, creating a dynamic and energetic atmosphere.
- **Musical Accompaniment:** Traditional Afghan music, including instruments like the *rubāb* (a lute like string instrument) and the *duhol* (a double-headed drum), may accompany *Buzkashi* matches. The lively melodies and rhythmic beats enhance the excitement and add a cultural dimension to the soundscape.
- **Crowd Reactions:** *Buzkashi* matches attract enthusiastic spectators who actively participate in the event. The crowd's cheers, applause, and exclamations contribute to the overall soundscape, reflecting the excitement, tension, and support for their favourite players.
- **Whips and Stirrups:** The players often use whips and stirrups to control their horses and manoeuvre during the game. The cracking sound of the whip and the clinking of stirrups against the horses' sides create distinctive sounds that are synonymous with *Buzkashi*.

It is important to know the timeline of every stage of the game and the layout of the sports ground to compose an audio track. The following figure by Azoy (1982, p. 118) gives an idea about the layout of the sports ground.

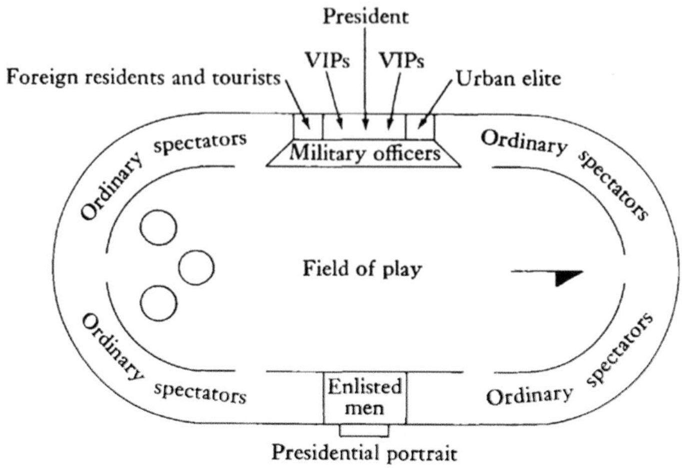

Figure 2.1 Seating arrangements and layout of audience in Kabul *Buzkashi* (Azoy, 1982, p. 118)

To effectively apply the soundscape of traditional sports like *Buzkashi* to video game audio design, developers need to prioritise an audio experience that mirrors the intensity of the sport in its cultural context. This can be achieved by layering authentic sounds, such as the thundering hooves of galloping horses, which should vary in intensity, depending on the speed and actions of the players. Adding vocalisations from the Chapandaz players will create an engaging atmosphere, so incorporating directional audio cues for shouts and calls can enhance strategic communication among players. Integrating traditional Afghan music which is commonly played during the event of *Buzkashi* at pivotal moments in the gameplay – not only in background tracks but also as reactive sound events when players achieve milestones – could deepen the cultural connection and emotional engagement. Additionally, real-time audio feedback from the enthusiastic crowd can reflect the game's ebb and flow, providing players with a palpable sense of support and competition.

Entertainment

Sound and music are integral components of various entertainment forms, significantly enhancing narrative, emotional depth, and overall immersive experiences. In film and television, soundtracks and sound design are critical in establishing mood, enhancing storytelling, and forging emotional connections with viewers. This principle also extends to theatre and live performances, where music, sound effects, and dialogue interact to craft a rich multisensory experience. Concerts and music festivals provide unique sonic environments where live performances and the collective energy of the audience create a memorable experience.

Sonic entertainment elements become emblematic of the culture's artistic expressions, traditions, and values, contributing to the cultural identity of a community. Carnivals in Brazil are known for their exuberant parades, colourful costumes, and lively music. The sonic elements of Brazilian carnivals include samba rhythms, brass instruments, and energetic vocals. These sounds represent the cultural identity of Brazil, celebrating the country's diverse heritage, the spirit of joy and celebration, and the importance of music and dance as expressions of Brazilian culture.

> These performances demonstrated that carnival is a flexible and living art form consisting of sonic, visual, and embodied elements that performers and directors re-contextualize freely. The performances also indicate significant links between identity politics, cultural performance, and the repurposing of strategic urban locations as entertainment zones in large cities throughout the world.
>
> (Gough, 2017, p. 119).

Entertainment in indigenous cultures is an interesting issue in sonic entertainment studies. Powwows, for instance, are gatherings of Native American communities that showcase traditional music, dance, and cultural expressions. The sonic elements of powwows include the beating of drums, the chanting and singing of Native American songs, and the rhythmic movements of traditional dances. These sounds contribute to the cultural identity of indigenous communities, preserving their ancestral traditions, spirituality, and sense of social belonging.

Sonic Ethnology of Everyday Activities and Household Sounds

While globalisation and technological advancements have led to the sharing of certain sounds and household sounds, such as kitchen applicants, phone ringing, doorbells, and so on across cultures, there are still distinct household sounds that remain specific to particular cultures and regions. These cultural-specific sounds often reflect the traditions, lifestyles, and daily activities of a particular community. They can be influenced by factors such as architecture, climate, social practices, and historical traditions. For instance, in Mediterranean countries, it is common to have a midday rest period called a siesta. During this time, you may hear quieter household sounds, such as light conversation or the sound of a fan or air conditioning.

Ceremonies in houses in East Asian cultures like traditional tea ceremony causes delicate sounds of brewing tea and pouring tea into cups during the ceremony. Some other household soundscapes in East Asian cultures include sizzling and clanging sounds from stir-frying dishes in a wok, the sound of slippers or shoes being taken off or put on at the entrance of the house, and soft tinkling sounds of bamboo wind chimes often hung near windows or balconies. In traditional Japanese architecture, doors are often designed to slide open and closed, creating a distinct sound experience compared to the hinged doors commonly found in Europe and the US. The sound produced by sliding doors adds a unique auditory element, reflecting the cultural and architectural differences between these styles.

In African culture the fire crackling, pots and pans clanging, and ingredients being chopped or ground, children playing, including laughter, shouts, and the sounds of games, footsteps, handclaps, and jingling sounds from ankle bells or other dance accessories are among everyday soundscape specific to African culture.

Some American Indian tribes have unique cooking methods or traditional dishes that involve specific sounds. For example, the preparation of traditional Navajo frybread may involve the sizzling sound of dough frying in oil. They also have a rich tradition of crafting traditional items, such as beadwork, pottery, or basketry. These crafts may involve specific sounds like the clinking of beads, the shaping of clay, or the weaving of fibres.

It should be noted that the examples presented here may not apply to the entire part of a region or tribe. The soundscape can be influenced by factors such as architecture, climate, social practices, and historical traditions. Yet, the matter of globalisation in shaping today's soundscapes of various cultures is an unresolved issue.

Soundwalk

Soundwalk is a method developed by soundscape researchers since the 1970s. In this method researchers individually or in the shape of a group walk along a site – usually urban common places like squares, bazaars, etc. – while recording the ambient sound from the environment in monthly or yearly periods to mark evaluation locations and audiovisual scenes on maps. One of the studies carrying out the methods and instances of soundwalks studies is Jeon, Hong, and Lee's in 2013 entitled "Soundwalk Approach to Identify Urban Soundscapes Individually." This study mostly deals with the acoustical issue rather than the ethnographical characteristics of the soundscape. However, providing the possibility to track the soundscape changes over time is the most valuable advantage of this method. Some scholars and artist soundwalkers sometimes take people's attitudes and viewpoints too which are very helpful in figuring out the humane sense of the recorded soundscape. The approach of soundwalk was later developed by Julien Tardieu and colleagues (2015) which was facilitated by laboratory tests to study the reaction of listeners, too.

Here is an example of a soundwalk in Valletta, capital of Malta, by Yiannis Christidis and Michael Quinton (2016, pp. 109–10):

> A soundwalk in Valletta begins from the immediate area outside the city walls, where the main bus terminus is, and one can hear buses leaving and parking constantly. The sound of spraying water from the Triton Fountain situated in the middle of the terminus covers the sound of the bus engines. All along the terminus area, there are kiosks selling food and drinks and people who are hanging around them chatting loudly. We walk over the bridge and venture into the city. There is a wave of people walking in either direction and one manages to hear bits of conversation. One can hear Maltese, English, Italian, Spanish, French, Russian, Serbian, African languages, probably Somali or Sudanese or some other. Passing the gate, on either side of Republic Street are two flights of stairs that go to the left and to the right away from the street. The din of chatter, footsteps and construction sound coming from the new parliament building that is still under construction, hangs in the air. Walking further down this main road, one can hear the odd busker. Peruvian pan pipes, acoustic guitars, opera singers, violinists, piano accordions and even an upright piano in front of the law courts where any passerby can sit down and play. And just across the piano, there are people who make and sell handicrafts. The musical fountain at St. Georges Square pulsates in rhythm to the music being played, accompanied by the gleeful laughter of children as they run through the water and parents snap photos or capture the fun on video. Walking away, one hears a car coming down one of the narrow side roads and turns down into Republic Street. The car passes and beeps its horn due to the amount of tourists and locals crossing at this point. Walking further down the road, the sound of the busy commercial and tourist part of the city starts to fade into the background and the street becomes quieter. There are steps that lead down the pavement and one can hear the irregular sound of footsteps due to the size of the steps which are low but long, not permitting one to go up or down in the regular sequential order of left and right. The rhythm goes: – down, step, step, down or up, step, step, up. The bottom of the Republic Street meets the surrounding ring road, which goes all around the city. One can hear coaches, minivans and taxis whizzing by and the sound of horses and coaches is a common sound characteristic in this part of the city. The Cabby calls to the passing tourists in a distinct tone and a broken English accent to see whether they want to tour around the city by horse and coach and that it will cost a certain amount of money.

Audio game designers can analyse the outcome of the captured soundwalks to create mood-matching sonic elements, utilising cultural symbols to evoke feelings linked to the represented culture. Experimental audio techniques, like sound manipulation and algorithmic composition inspired by the patterns observed during soundwalks, can further enhance gameplay. Contextualising audio to reflect specific cultural practices and narratives offers players insights into the culture within the game.

Aural Postcards

One of the scholars who thought of the sound of cities as an aural postcard is Walter Benjamin (1925, p. 82):

> The special sense of a city may be no longer is given by tower-clocks and church-bells – by sounds, that is, which tell time – but rather by those that tell of motion. The peculiar sounds of transit are the signature tunes of modern cities. These are sounds that remind us the city is a sort of machine.

He suggests that

> The diesel stammer of London taxis, the wheeze of its buses. The clatter of the Melbourne tram. The two-stroke sputter of Rome. The note that sounds as the doors shut on the Paris metro, and the flick, flick, flick of the handles.
>
> (Benjamin, 1925, p. 82)

are kept as souvenirs of those places just similar to handicrafts and postcards.

Fran Tonkiss (2020) suggests the idea of aural postcards in the study of the urban soundscape. He compares the aural postcards to conventional visual postcards. A postcard has a front and back. The front is normally a recognisable printed picture of a place. The back, however, is often the handwriting of a personal note. The aural postcards have a parallel sense of public versus private experience. On the front side of an aural postcard, we can listen to a general soundscape of an area. This includes sounds that any person of the general public would hear at the place at hand in the particular postcard. Any aural postcard has a backside, too, which is more personal and very much depends on the individual's perception. The backside has meanings that can evoke definite memories that matter to certain individuals or social groups which may never be understood by outsiders who had never experienced such memories. The night of a city is not just a dark picture of that city, which flashing lights of billboards, shops, and pobs bring a different image of the city; the aural postcard of that city also significantly differs from the daytime aural postcard.

In video games, the soundscape serves as the front side of the aural postcard. The environmental sounds contribute to an overall atmosphere that defines the game world – just as a bustling city might present the sounds of traffic, chatter, and music, a game may have ambient sounds that immerse the player in a distinct environment. For example, the chirping of crickets and rustling leaves in a forest or the distant sirens and honking horns of an urban setting establish a recognisable backdrop. These sounds function as familiar touchpoints for players, creating an auditory call to place that resonates with their experiences of those environments, reflective of cultural or geographical contexts.

The nuanced, individual response to game audio parallels the personal note on the back of a postcard. Players engage with these soundscapes not just as passive listeners but as active participants whose interpretations can be shaped by their personal histories, cultural backgrounds, and emotional states. For example, the lamenting voice of a tragic event in a game may evoke personal memories of loss, while combat sounds might catalyse adrenaline and excitement shaped by one's past experiences with competitive play. Just as a non-player may not grasp the layers of meaning in the audio nuances of a seasoned player, those unfamiliar with gaming may find it challenging to understand the emotional depth that audio can convey.

Special Day vs. Everyday

Sound is capable of marking out a special day from ordinary days. When shops downtown close down and streets become empty because everyone has to attend a ceremony at the cathedral, we can hear the birds singing on trees and woodpeckers drilling holes in trees to store acorns and other nature sounds we can never hear during working days. In the weeks leading up to Easter prior to Ash Wednesday carnivals with parades, masquerade balls, entertainment, music, and parties passing by every street in towns and cities in Italy, we can no longer hear the everyday soundscape of the city. Italians say *"a Carnevale ogni scherzo vale,"* which means "anything goes at Carnival."

In disasters, including earthquakes, volcanic eruptions, landslides, tsunamis, floods, drought, war, and pandemic diseases, the sound of the cities changes intensely:

> In Freetown, Sierra Leone, one hears the droning of the military helicopter overhead watching. This is in stark contrast to the silence of the deserted streets below – with large sections of the population quarantined, curfewed or afraid to go out onto the streets for fear of contracting Ebola. Between the silence of the streets and throbbing noise from above comes the wailing of the sirens of ambulances as they slowly and interminably make their way over the gravel and pitted tracks of the street in order to pick up their deadly cargo of the corpses of the victims of Ebola, wrapped in plastic body bags to be deposited in graves beyond the eyes and touch of their loved ones. The sirens denote the end of the culture of dying – with

> its attendant rituals that signify the value of life and community – and the coming together of the living to respect and remember the dead.
>
> (Bull & Back, 2020, p. 10)

During the coronavirus lockdown, the soundscape of cities changed. Stuart Fowkes has been mapping sounds from across the world since 2014 as a way to track how they change over time. He noticed that since the lockdown of the pandemic Covid 19 imposed in 2020, the manmade sounds lowered so that the sound of nature found a chance to be heard again. Fowkes noticed that the sounds that are unique to a city but that had been lost to noise pollution over the years prior to the pandemic of Covid 19, such as birds, insects, and other elements of nature, and the ringing of church bells and so on, became audible again.

There is an endless number of manmade sounds caused by industry and workstations, busyness, sports, entertainment, and household sounds which may be included in the soundtrack of video games and have to be in accordance with geographical and cultural context.

Practical Matters

Creating a realistic soundscape in a video game can greatly enhance the immersion and overall player experience. I categorise general elements you can consider incorporating to capture the essence of soundscapes here. You need to consider the cultural contexts in designing every soundscape as examined in this chapter:

Ambiance

Start with a background ambiance that reflects the specific type of the venue. For example, an office environment could feature the sounds of keyboards tapping, printers humming, distant conversations, and occasional phone rings. A factory or workshop might have machinery operating, clanking tools, and echoing footsteps. When designing audio tracks for ambiance soundscapes, there are several important factors to consider, including

- **Sound Sources:** Identify the primary sound sources that are present in the venue.
- **Context and Setting:** Consider the location, time period, and any relevant cultural or environmental factors.
- **Purpose, Mood, and Emotional Impact:** Determine the purpose and desired mood of the soundscape. Are you aiming for a peaceful and serene ambiance or a tense and suspenseful one? The choice of sounds and their arrangement can evoke different emotional responses from the listeners.

- **Timing and Variation:** Create a sense of realism by incorporating timing and variation in the soundscape. Introduce variations and randomisation to make the soundscape feel more dynamic and natural. This will prevent the ambiance from sounding monotonous and repetitive.
- **Layering:** Use multiple layers of sounds to create depth and complexity. Combine various elements, such as background sounds, specific environmental sounds, and character interactions.
- **Spatial Placement:** Use panning and volume adjustments to position sounds in different areas of the stereo or surround sound field.
- **Transition and Looping:** Smooth transitions help maintain a seamless audio experience. When designing an ambiance track, ensure that it can be seamlessly looped for continuous playback. This is particularly important when the ambiance is used as background audio for extended periods.
- **Timbre and Dynamics:** Different environments have different timbre and dynamic characteristics. Considering the timbre and dynamic atmospheres give a lively feeling to the game players.
- **Environmental Interactions:** Think about how the environment and objects within it can interact with sounds.
- **Player Interaction:** Consider how player actions and interactions can affect the ambiance soundscape.
- **Technical Limitations:** Keep in mind any technical limitations of the platform or game engine you're working with. Consider file size, processing power, and memory constraints to ensure your audio tracks are optimised for performance.

Footsteps

Implement different footstep sounds to match the flooring materials found in the location. For instance, carpeted areas may produce soft and muffled footsteps, while concrete floors could create more distinct and reverberating sounds. Covering the floor greatly relates to the cultures and environments. It is obvious to find wooden floors in forest homes and workplaces and stone floors in mountains. Tribal Arabs in deserts cover their floor with carpets woven by leaves of palm dates trees and wools of camels. Iranians use Persian carpets for flooring places.

Interactions

Audio cues play a crucial role in enhancing player immersion and engagement. Sounds associated with specific actions – such as picking up or moving objects – are not merely background elements; they serve as essential feedback mechanisms that inform players about their environment and the interactions they are performing. For instance, the clattering of coins when a player gathers treasure or the rustle of leaves as they navigate through a forest each creates a more vivid and believable world for players to experience. Such audio cues can significantly enrich the narrative and emotional impact of gameplay.

Utilising generic sound effects from readily available archives without considering their cultural implications can lead to misrepresentation and a lack of authenticity. Designing custom sound effects can offer a tailored approach that speaks directly to the themes and settings of your game. It can help creating sounds that resonate authentically with the cultural elements you want to highlight, ensuring that your game's audio is not only immersive but also respectful and representative.

By recording sounds directly from a specific location or culture, you can capture the unique auditory essence that generic sound effects simply cannot provide. For example, if your game is set in a rural village in Japan, capturing the sound of traditional wooden clogs on tatami mats or the distant call of a temple bell would significantly elevate the player's experience, allowing them to feel as if they are truly part of that world.

Conversations

Incorporate snippets of conversations among non-playable characters (NPCs) or colleagues. This can make the workplace feel alive and dynamic. Consider using a mix of intelligible speech and indistinct murmuring to create a realistic backdrop. In situations of multicultural environments try to use languages that are spoken most in that region. For instance, you may find lots of Chinese people in New York, but you may scarcely find any Chinese in Baghdad. However, Kurdish and Persian speakers may be heard a lot in Baghdad, where the official language is Arabic.

As you step into the bustling workplace, the air is filled with a mix of intelligible speech and indistinct murmuring, creating a lively and dynamic atmosphere. Colleagues engage in conversations, and snippets of their discussions weave together to form a realistic backdrop. In this multicultural environment, where different languages resonate with the regions they represent, you can hear a variety of voices. Look at the following example in a vibrant Baghdad workplace:

Colleague 1 (speaking Arabic): "أوعدتك أن تصلح هذا العطل. متى يمكننا أن نتوقع أن تكون الأمور على ما يرام؟" (Translation: "You promised to fix this issue. When can we expect things to be back on track?")

Colleague 2 (speaking Kurdish): "باشە! من ئەولەویەتی دادەنێم و دەست دەکەم بە کارکردن لەسەر ئەرکەکانم." (Translation: "Alright! I'll prioritise it and get to work on my tasks.")

Colleague 3 (speaking Persian): "بله حتماً. من تا ظهر فرصت دارم و به شما کمک می‌کنم." (Translation: "Certainly. I have some time until noon, and I'll assist you.")

The surrounding conversations blend together, echoing the cultural diversity of the workplace, as colleagues collaborate and navigate their daily tasks.

Equipment and Tools

Depending on the nature of the place, you can include sounds associated with specific equipment or tools. For example, a construction site might feature the rumble of heavy machinery, the whir of power tools, or the clanging of metal. As a case think of a traditional sailing ship in Morocco. You would find a variety of equipment and tools that contribute to the unique soundscape on board. The sound effects would include

- Rigging sounds: The ship's rigging consists of ropes, lines, and pulleys used to control the sails. As the wind catches the sails, you may hear the creaking and straining of the rigging, accompanied by the rattling of blocks and shackles.
- Sails flapping: When the wind changes direction or intensity, the sails may flap as they adjust. This creates a distinct rustling sound as the canvas catches the air.
- Wind whistling: As the ship picks up speed, the wind passing through the rigging and the sails can produce a soft, melodic whistling sound.
- Anchor chains: When dropping or raising the anchor, you might hear the clinking and clanking of heavy anchor chains as they are released or pulled in.
- Helm and rudder: The helmsman steers the ship using a large wooden helm connected to the rudder. Turning the helm creates a creaking sound as the wooden components move against each other.
- Oars and rowlocks: In smaller traditional sailing vessels, oars may be used for propulsion. The rhythmic splashing and dipping of the oars in the water, accompanied by the subtle creaking of the rowlocks, create a distinctive soundscape.
- Bilge pumps: Traditional sailing ships often have manual bilge pumps used to remove water from the hull. These pumps produce a repetitive pumping sound when operated.
- Deck activities: On board, you may hear sounds associated with various activities, such as crew members walking on the wooden deck, the clanging of tools used for maintenance and repairs, or the sound of ropes being coiled or uncoiled.
- Bells and whistles: Traditional sailing ships often have bells or whistles used for signalling or communicating important information to the crew. The ringing of bells or blowing of whistles can punctuate the soundscape.
- Voices and chatter: The voices and conversations of the crew members in Arabic and Berber languages, along with their laughter and occasional shouts of command, contribute to the lively soundscape of a traditional sailing ship.

The combination of these sounds creates a unique and atmospheric experience that varies depending on the ship's size, design, and the specific activities taking place at the time.

Environmental Factors

Consider how environmental factors can affect the soundscape. For instance, if the workplace has large windows, you might include the sound of rain or distant traffic. If the location is near an airport, you could incorporate occasional airplane noises. Review again the issues raised in chapter one, "Sound of the Nature," to build a successful environmental sound effect track.

Background Music

To further enhance the atmosphere, you can add background music that complements the workplace setting. Choose music that is appropriate for the tone and mood you want to convey, whether it is relaxed and ambient or intense and fast-paced. Later in this volume, there will be a chapter on music which will help you build appropriate music for every scene.

Spatial Audio

Implementing spatial audio techniques can greatly enhance the realism of the workplace soundscape, creating an immersive auditory experience. Spatial audio involves the creation and reproduction of sound in a way that simulates its real-world spatial properties. It aims to replicate how sound behaves in physical environments, including direction, distance, and reflections. Here are some steps to help you implement spatial audio techniques in the case of a traditional bazaar in Istanbul. Implementing spatial audio techniques to exemplify a bazaar in Istanbul can create an immersive auditory experience, replicating the bustling and vibrant atmosphere of such a place. Here are the steps:

- Understand the bazaar environment: Familiarise yourself with the typical sounds and characteristics of a bazaar in Istanbul. Research the ambiance, such as the sounds of vendors, customers, haggling, footsteps, and other unique elements that contribute to the atmosphere.
- Capture or create spatial audio content: To create spatial audio content, you can either capture real-world audio recordings in an actual bazaar or create them using audio production software. Consider using omnidirectional or ambisonic microphones to capture the audio from various directions and capture the overall ambiance.
- Identify key audio sources: Determine the key audio sources that contribute to the bazaar soundscape, such as vendors calling out, the clinking of

tea glasses, or the sound of footsteps on cobblestones. These sources will be spatialised and positioned accordingly to create an accurate representation of the bazaar.

- Position and orient audio sources: Based on the bazaar environment, determine the location and orientation of each audio source within the virtual space. Place the sources at appropriate positions, considering the layout of the bazaar and the distance between different elements.
- Encode spatial audio: Choose an audio format that supports spatial audio, such as ambisonics or object-based audio. Encode the captured or created audio content with spatial information, assigning proper metadata to each audio source to represent its position, orientation, and other relevant parameters.
- Select a playback system: Choose a playback system that supports spatial audio rendering, such as headphones or loudspeaker arrays. Ensure the system can accurately reproduce the spatial properties of the encoded audio.
- Configure playback setup: Set up the playback system according to the manufacturer's instructions. Calibrate the loudspeaker positions or adjust headphone settings to match the desired spatial audio rendering.
- Test and refine: Play back the spatial audio content and evaluate its realism and accuracy in representing the bazaar environment. Make adjustments as needed, such as refining the position and orientation of audio sources or adjusting room acoustic parameters, to enhance the overall experience.
- Consider additional elements: To further enhance the realism, you can incorporate additional elements like reverberation or room acoustic effects that simulate the specific acoustic characteristics of a bazaar. This can help create a more convincing auditory environment.
- Integrate with visuals: If you are creating a virtual reality or augmented reality experience, integrate the spatial audio techniques with the visual elements to provide a fully immersive and synchronised experience. Ensure that the audio aligns with the virtual environment, user movements, and visual cues.

It is important to balance the volume levels of different sound elements to ensure they do not overwhelm or distract players. Additionally, consider providing options for players to adjust the volume of specific sound elements or mute them if they prefer.

Chapter 3

Language Structure and Speech Styles

Introduction

"Culture is in language, and language is loaded with culture" (Agar, 2007, p. 23). Research on the ethnography of language, impacting both linguistics and linguistic anthropology, began with Dell Hymes' influential work in 1974. Hymes examined the societal norms of speech communities as essential for understanding the meaning of words in specific contexts. This approach was further developed by Stephen Levinson in his comprehensive exploration of pragmatics in 1983, where he criticised speech act theory and highlighted the importance of analysing speech acts within conversational contexts to address longstanding issues in the field. Levinson emphasised that a contextualised study of speech acts, considering their placement within conversations, is necessary for resolving challenges in speech act theory. Geoffrey Leech (1983) highlighted the importance of considering the face of the listener in addition to the speaker in utterance production/interpretation.

Penelope Brown and Levinson (1987) further explored politeness as a universal strategy to protect the face of listeners, particularly through indirect speech acts that avoid imposing obligations on them. It is followed by the works of Holmes (2013), Eelen (2001), Mills (2003), Watts (2003), and Culpeper (2011) and recent scholars in the field (Capone & Mey, 2015, p. 4).

The structure of every language involves several factors, including grammar, vocabulary, pronunciation and idioms. In a micro-analysis of a language, we may look at the structure of words and phrases and what makes them, including phonemes, morphemes, lexemes, syntax, and context. They provide a unique way for people to express their thoughts, ideas, and emotions, and they can reflect the values, beliefs, and customs that play a significant role in shaping the identity of culture.

"If you focus only on the similarities between languages, you miss out on all of the exciting ways in which they differ" (Aronoff & Fudeman, 2011, p. 9). The vocabulary of a language is a reflection of the distinct cultural practices and experiences of a community. For example, a language that has a large number of words related to agriculture may indicate that the

DOI: 10.4324/9781003591399-4

community has a strong connection to the land and a history of working in agriculture. The grammar of a language can also reflect the cultural values and beliefs of a community. For example, a language that places a strong emphasis on politeness and respect may indicate that the culture places a high value on interpersonal relationships. The pronunciation of a language can vary significantly depending on the culture. For example, some cultures may have a more melodic and sing-song style of speaking, while others may have a more straightforward style of speaking.

Idioms are expressions or phrases that have a figurative meaning that is different from the literal meaning of the words. Idioms can reflect the history and traditions of a culture. For example, many English idioms have their roots in historical events or cultural practices, such as "raining cats and dogs" or "barking up the wrong tree." Idioms may also reflect the values and beliefs of a culture. For example, in many cultures, there are idioms that emphasise the importance of hard work or perseverance, such as "no pain, no gain" or "when the going gets tough, the tough get going." These idioms reflect the value that is placed on determination and resilience in those cultures. The use of idioms specific to a particular culture or language creates a sense of connection and mutual understanding among people.

The terms "low-context culture" (LCC) and "high-context culture" (HCC) were created by Hall to describe how communication styles differ across cultures. In LCC, meaning is expressed through explicit verbal messages, both written and oral. In HCC, on the other hand, intention or meaning can best be conveyed through implicit contexts, including gestures, social customs, silence, nuance, or tone of voice. You may be wondering, by this point, how low-context and high-context cultures differ across different countries. Japan, UAE, Brazil, and Italy are among high-context cultures countries, and Swiss, Germany and Sweden enjoy low-cultural context communications (Wrench et al., 2020).

> When a husband comes home from the office, takes off his hat, hangs up his coat, and says "Hi" to his wife, the way in which he says "Hi," reinforced by the manner in which he sheds his overcoat, summarizes his feelings about the way things went at the office. If his wife wants the details she may have to listen for a while, yet she grasps in an instant the significant message for her; namely, what kind of evening they are going to spend and how she is going to have to cope with it.
>
> (Hall, 1959, p. 121)

The distinction between low-context and high-context communication is crucial when designing audio for video games. In games aimed at audiences from low-context cultures, the use of explicit verbal cues and clear audio signals is essential to effectively convey vital information regarding character emotions and plot developments. This approach ensures that players receive information without ambiguity. In contrast, for games targeting high-context culture audiences, sound design can employ more subtle audio elements, such as nuanced background ambient sounds, and character vocal tones. These elements allow for a more implicit conveyance of emotions and narrative developments, enabling players to derive meaning from context and nuance.

Phonetics and Phonology

Phonology deals with how speech sounds are organised into systems in every language; for example, how the sounds can be combined, related, and affect each other (Davenport & Hannahs, 2010, p. 237). Phonetics deals with speech sounds, how they are made (articulatory phonetics), how they are perceived (auditory phonetics), and the physics involved (acoustic phonetics). A combination of accent, pronunciation, phonemic inventory, and onomatopoeia can contribute to the identity of different cultures in several ways. The way a language is pronounced, including variations in accent, intonation, and speech rhythm, can be closely tied to a particular culture or region. These phonetic features can serve as markers of identity, distinguishing speakers from different geographical areas or social groups. For example, the distinctive accents of English spoken in the United States, the United Kingdom, and Australia are often associated with their respective cultures. Moreover, each language has a unique set of phonemes.

The phonemic inventory of a language can reflect cultural aspects such as the sounds considered significant or important in that culture. For instance, certain languages may have phonemes that do not exist in other languages, reflecting the specific speech patterns and cultural context of the community that speaks that language.

Onomatopoeic words, which imitate sounds, are often influenced by the phonetic system of a language. Different cultures may have distinct onomatopoeic words based on their phonetic repertoire. For example, the sound of a dog barking may be represented as "woof" in English, "wan wan" in Japanese, "wāgh wāgh" in Persian or "guau guau" in Spanish. These variations reflect both linguistic and cultural differences.

In a structural sense, linguists are interested in how phonetics shapes in every language. In the English language for instance, we cannot distinguish between two different words in English by replacing for example one "t" sound with another "t" sound: having a "t" without aspiration (like the one in "stuck") at the beginning of "tuck" does not give us a different English word (it just gives us a slightly odd pronunciation of the same word, "tuck"). Replacing the "t" with a "d," clearly does result in a different English word: "duck." So where phonetically there are four different sounds, phonologically there are only two contrasting elements, the "t" and the "d" (Davenport & Hannahs, 2010, p. 237).

Phonology includes the study of phonemes, intonation, stress, and rhythm. Phonemes are the smallest units of sound in a language, and they play a crucial role in language structure. A phoneme is a distinct sound that can change the meaning of a word when it is replaced with another phoneme. For example, in English, the phonemes /p/ and /b/ are distinct sounds that can change the meaning of a word, as in "pat" and "bat." Phonemes can also play a role in cultural identity. The way that phonemes are pronounced can vary between different languages and dialects, and this can be a marker of cultural identity. For example, the way that certain consonants are pronounced in Arabic can be a marker of regional identity. Similarly, the way that vowels are pronounced in different dialects of English can be a marker of cultural identity. In addition to being a marker of cultural identity, phonemes can also be used to create new words and expressions in a language. For example, in English, the phonemes /sk/ and /r/ can be combined to create the word "scare," which has a different meaning than the words "scar" or "share." This ability to form new words and meanings through phonemes plays a crucial role in the evolution of language.

In the development of video game audio, the diverse onomatopoeic representations of sounds can guide the selection of sound effects that are both linguistically and culturally appropriate, facilitating a deeper connection between players and the game. In the following section, I will conduct a phonological comparison between English and Spanish to highlight the issues mentioned above.

A Phonological Compression Between English and Spanish

I compare the phonological aspects of English and Spanish languages by presenting some examples. It includes differences in consonants, vowels, and stresses. English has a wide range of consonant sounds, including voiced and voiceless stops, fricatives, affricates, nasals, and liquids. Spanish also has a variety of consonant sounds, but the inventory is slightly different from English.

English Consonants (e.g.)	*Spanish Consonants (e.g.)*
- /p/ as in "pat"	- /p/ as in "pato" (duck)
- /s/ as in "sit"	- /s/ as in "sol" (sun)
- /tʃ/ as in "church"	- /tʃ/ as in "chico" (boy)
- /m/ as in "mat"	- /m/ as in "mano" (hand)
- /l/ as in "let"	- /l/ as in "luz" (light)

English has a relatively complex vowel system with several pure vowels (monophthongs) and diphthongs. Spanish has a simpler vowel system compared to English, with five pure vowels (monophthongs) and no diphthongs.

English Vowels	*Spanish Vowels*
- /i/ as in "see" - /ɛ/ as in "bed" - /aɪ/ as in "ride" - /ʊ/ as in "book" - /ɔɪ/ as in "boy"	- /i/ as in "piso" (floor) - /e/ as in "perro" (dog) - /a/ as in "casa" (house) - /o/ as in "gato" (cat) - /u/ as in "luna" (moon)

English is a stress-timed language, which means that stressed syllables are typically pronounced with more emphasis and duration. English has complex syllable structures, allowing for consonant clusters at the beginning and end of syllables. Spanish is a syllable-timed language, where each syllable tends to have an equal duration. Spanish has simpler syllable structures compared to English, with fewer consonant clusters.

Examples of stresses in English	*Examples of stress in Spanish*
- *"beach" /biːtʃ/ (1 syllable)* - *"pencil" /ˈpɛnsəl/ (2 syllables)* - *"elephant" /ˈɛlɪfənt/ (3 syllables)* - *"banana" /bəˈnænə/ (3 syllables)*	- *"sol" /sol/ (1 syllable)* - *"casa" /ˈka.sa/ (2 syllables)* - *"elefante" /e.leˈfan.te/ (4 syllables)* - *"manzana" /man.ˈsa.na/ (3 syllables)*

There are other phonological differences between English and Spanish that I did not mention above, among them are "rhoticity" and "nasalisation." English is a rhotic language, meaning that speakers pronounce the /r/ sound in all contexts. Spanish, on the other hand, is a non-rhotic language and does not pronounce the /r/ sound after vowels. Regarding nasalisation, English speakers make nasal sounds like /m/ and /n/, while Spanish speakers do not normally use nasalised sounds.

Understanding the distinctions between consonantal and vowel systems is crucial for audio designers in selecting suitable voice actors, thereby ensuring that character dialogues authentically reflect their cultural contexts. Moreover, the differing stress patterns and syllabic structures play a significant role in the delivery of dialogue within the game, directly influencing pacing, emotional resonance, and overall player engagement. By leveraging insights gained from these phonological analyses, developers can refine their localisation strategies, ultimately making games more accessible and enjoyable for a diverse audience (for further details, refer to the localisation section).

Syntax

The syntax of a language refers to the set of rules and principles governing how words and phrases are organised and combined to form meaningful sentences. It includes the study of word order, sentence structure, and grammatical relationships between words. Syntax tends to be very regular, but the morphology is full of irregulations and exceptions (Aronoff & Fudeman, 2011, p. 159).

Syntax plays an important role in language structure as it allows speakers to convey complex ideas and relationships between words. Sentence structure may not seem to have an identity impact in a culture at first glance, but a closer look may reveal how such a phenomenon of language may give identity to its speakers. The way that sentences are structured and the order in which words are arranged can reflect cultural values, beliefs, and practices. For example, in some cultures, there may be a strong emphasis on expressing respect or politeness through the use of certain grammatical structures or honorifics. In other cultures, there may be a greater focus on directness and clarity in communication, which may be reflected in different sentence structures. The syntax can also be used to create new expressions and idioms that reflect cultural identity. For example, in some cultures, there may be idioms or expressions that are based on sentence structures that are unique to that culture.

Some languages have a subject-verb-object (SVO) word order, while others may have a subject-object-verb (SOV) or a verb-subject-object (VSO) word order. These structural differences can affect the way ideas are expressed and understood, and they can reflect cultural norms and preferences.

I compare the structure of sentences in English, Hindi and Persian here as an interesting case. In English, the basic word order is typically subject-verb-object (SVO), while in Hindi and Persian, it is subject-object-verb (SOV). This means that in Hindustani and Persian, the verb usually comes at the end of the sentence. Similar to English, adjectives in Hindustani typically come before the noun they modify, but in Persian, it comes after the noun. In Hindi adverbs can come before or after the verb, similar to English. Question word order in Hindustani is formed by placing the question word, such as "where," at the beginning of the sentence, followed by the verb and subject, while maintaining the basic SOV word order. However, in Persian, the question words come at the end of the sentence just before the verb.

English	*Hindi*	*Persian*
1. Subject-Verb-Object (SVO) word order: "She eats an apple."	1. Subject-Object-Verb (SOV) word order: "वह एक सेब खाती है" (She an apple eats).	1. Subject-Object-Verb (SOV) word order: "او یک سیب می‌خورد" (She an apple eats).
2. Adjective-Noun word order: "Big house."	2. Adjective-Noun word order: "बड़ा घर" (Big house).	2. Noun-Adjective word order: "خانه بزرگ" (house big).
3. Adverb-verb word order: "Quickly run!"	3. Adverb-Verb word order: "तेज़ी से दौड़ो!" (Quickly run!).	3. Adverb-Verb word order: "تند بدو" (Quickly run!).
4. Question word order: "Where is the library?"	4. Question word order: "पुस्तकालय कहाँ है?" (Library where is?).	4. Question word order: "کتابخانه کجا است؟" (Library where is?).

Languages may have specific grammatical constructions or verb forms to express politeness or honorifics, indicating the importance placed on social hierarchies and respect. Indeed, languages may have grammatical categories or structures that reflect cultural concepts, such as collectivism, individualism, or gender roles.

The syntax of a language can influence how cultural practices and events are described and conveyed. Different cultures may have specific linguistic structures or sentence patterns to express rituals, customs, or traditional activities. For example, a language may have specific verb forms or temporal markers to describe ceremonial events or religious practices, reflecting the cultural significance of these activities.

Another issue to be bear in video game designing is the impact of the syntax of languages on the structure and nature of storytelling. The syntax of a language can influence the way stories, narratives, and folklore are structured and conveyed. In games that utilise branching narratives or player-driven dialogue systems, the syntax of the language can dictate how choices are framed and perceived by players.

Syntactic structures affect the rhythm and pacing of dialogues. A language with a more flexible syntax might allow for longer, more complex sentences that create a dense, immersive storytelling experience, whereas a language with a more rigid structure might favour brevity and clarity, necessitating a different pacing in narrative delivery. Moreover, language syntax can affect character development and depth. A language that encourages indirect speech or nuanced expression may allow characters to convey subtleties of emotion and intent, impacting player perception and engagement. If a game is localised from one language to another, variations in syntax might require adjustments in character dialogue to maintain the same level of emotional resonance and realistic interaction. When adapting a game for different linguistic markets, understanding the syntactical idiosyncrasies of a target language becomes crucial. Translators and designers must navigate the syntactical structure to preserve narrative integrity while ensuring that dialogue remains natural and relatable for the new audience. Failure to account for these differences can lead to flat or confused narrative experiences that detract from player engagement.

Lexeme

A lexeme is a word with a specific sound and a specific meaning. Its shape may vary depending on syntactic context (Aronoff & Fudeman, 2011, p. 43). It is a basic unit of meaning in a language, and it includes all the inflected forms of a word, such as its base form, plurals, verb tenses, and so on. For example, the lexeme "run" includes all its inflected forms, such as "runs," "running," "ran," and "will run." Each of these forms represents the same basic meaning of the lexeme, which is "to move quickly on foot." By identifying

Table 3.1 Lexemes in Spanish and Chinese

	Lexemes in Spanish	*Lexemes in Chinese*
Word structure:	Spanish lexemes typically consist of a root or stem, with affixes added to modify the meaning or grammatical function. Spanish has a rich system of inflectional suffixes that indicate aspects like tense, number, gender, and case.	Chinese lexemes are primarily monosyllabic, meaning that each character typically represents a single morpheme or lexeme. Chinese words are often formed by combining different characters to create compound words. Chinese does not have a complex system of inflectional morphology like Spanish.
Grammatical Categories:	Spanish lexemes inflect to indicate grammatical categories such as gender (masculine/feminine) and number (singular/plural). Verbs also inflect for tense, aspect, mood, and person.	Chinese lexemes do not have extensive inflectional morphology to indicate grammatical categories like gender or number. Instead, word order and function words play a crucial role in expressing grammatical relationships and meaning.
Character vs. Alphabet:	Spanish lexemes are typically written using the Latin alphabet. Each letter represents a specific sound, and the combination of letters forms words.	Chinese lexemes are represented by characters, with each character often representing a morpheme or a whole lexeme. Chinese characters are logograms, and the meaning of a character is often related to its visual representation.
Lexical Ambiguity	Spanish lexemes can sometimes have multiple meanings depending on the context, but the ambiguity is usually resolved through grammar or additional words.	Chinese lexemes are susceptible to homophony and homography, as many characters may have the same pronunciation or similar appearance. The context is crucial in disambiguating the meaning of lexemes in Chinese.

the lexeme of a word, linguists can see how different forms of the word are related to each other and how they are used in different contexts. Lexemes can also be used to identify the meanings of words in different languages. By comparing the lexemes of similar words in different languages, linguists can identify patterns and relationships between languages and understand how they are related. The main problem of lexical semantics is that the meanings of individual lexemes are highly diverse. It causes a potential communication problem called polysemy (Aronoff & Fudeman, 2011, p. 44). "Polysemy is a situation in which the same word has two or more different meanings" (Ullman, 1962, p. 159). For example, the term flight may refer to all of the following: "(i) the power of flying; (ii) an air journey; (iii) a series of steps; (iv) a digression; (v) a unit of air force" (Finch, 2000, p. 173). As a case, the lexemes in Spanish and Chinese are compared here.

Lexical choices often reflect the unique cultural experiences, values, and concepts of a community. Different cultures may have specific words to describe aspects of their traditions, beliefs, social structures, or natural environment. For example, words related to snow and ice are abundant in the Inuit language, reflecting their close relationship with the Arctic environment. Lexemes can include references to historical events, figures, or specific geographical locations that hold cultural significance. Such words evoke a sense of shared history, identity, and heritage among speakers of a language. For instance, words related to historical events or influential leaders can symbolise cultural pride and resilience. Words associated with traditional clothing, cuisine, music, dance, or religious ceremonies are intrinsic to a particular culture. These lexemes not only describe but also preserve and transmit cultural knowledge across generations.

Cross-cultural relations shape and modify lexemes around the globe. Languages often borrow words from other cultures, reflecting historical interactions, trade, colonisation, or globalisation. These borrowed words, known as loanwords, can indicate cultural influences, adaptations, or assimilation. For example, English has borrowed many words from French, reflecting the historical influence of the French language on English-speaking cultures.

Understanding idioms, proverbs, and expressions which are deeply rooted in culture often requires familiarity with the associated cultural context. This familiarity enables speakers to express themselves in culturally meaningful ways. Lexemes serve as mirrors to societal taboos, social norms, and conventions of politeness. Certain words may be considered offensive or inappropriate in a given culture, while others may be used to show respect, deference, or politeness.

Semantics

Semantics refers to the study of the meaning of language and how words and sentences convey meaning. It includes the study of word meanings, connotations, and denotations. The meanings of words and expressions can reflect cultural values, beliefs, and practices. For example, in some cultures, a strong emphasis may be placed on communal worship and collective rituals, reflecting a belief in the importance of the community in nurturing faith. In contrast, other cultures may prioritise individual spirituality and personal reflection, valuing personal connection with the divine over communal practices. In some cultures, the use of formal language and honorifics when referring to deities or spiritual leaders underscores a profound sense of respect and reverence. Alternatively, in other cultures, more casual or personal language may be utilised, reflecting a belief in accessibility and a close personal relationship with the divine. Moreover, the creation of new expressions or idioms that reflect religious values can signify cultural identity. For example, in some cultures, there may be religious phrases or proverbs that encapsulate key moral teachings, which may be unique to that culture and challenging to convey in other linguistic frameworks.

In some cultures, there may be a great focus on the use of metaphor or symbolism to convey meaning. Semantics can also be used to create new expressions and idioms that reflect cultural identity. For example, in some cultures, there may be expressions or words that are unique to that culture and cannot be fully translated into other languages.

Words can carry cultural connotations that go beyond their literal definitions. These connotations arise from the cultural associations and experiences attached to certain words. For instance, the word "home" may have different connotations in different cultures, representing not just a physical dwelling but also emotional attachments, family relationships, and a sense of belonging. Semantic patterns and expressions can reflect cultural scripts. Cultural scripts refer to shared knowledge and expectations about how certain situations or interactions should unfold within a specific culture. For example,

> the English word *generous* carries with a certain cognitive scenario and a positive evolution. This identifies for the speaker of English a cultural norm which at a certain level can be spelled out like this: "it is good if someone is generous."
>
> (Wierzbicka, 2015, p. 341)

Cultural interactions and influences can lead to the borrowing of semantic concepts and meanings between languages. In the field of music, Italian terms such as "allegro," "adagio," and "fortissimo" are commonly used in various languages to describe tempo and dynamics in musical pieces. These terms have been borrowed from Italian due to the substantial influence of Italian composers and music theorists in the development of Western classical music. When a concept or meaning is borrowed from one culture to another, it can shape and influence the cultural identity of the borrowing culture. For example, Italian opera has had a significant impact on the development of vocal music in many cultures, leading to the adoption of Italian terms, such as "aria," "recitative," and "libretto" in various languages. The borrowing of these technical music terms from Italian has not only enriched the musical vocabulary of other languages but has also contributed to the global spread of Italian musical traditions.

Video games often need to be localised for different regions, which includes translating dialogue and ensuring that contextual meanings and idioms resonate with the target audience. Certain phrases may have cultural significance or connotations that do not translate directly. Moreover, the choice of voice actors and their accents can heavily influence a game's reception. A character voiced in a culturally relevant way can enhance immersion, while a mismatch may lead to disconnection or misunderstanding. Familiarity with nestled meanings is another issue to bear in mind. Sounds associated with specific actions (such as a sword being drawn) may resonate differently based on cultural backgrounds. In one culture, this may be viewed as heroic, while in another, it might be perceived as an aggressive or negative act.

Pragmatics

Pragmatics refers to the study of how language is used in context and how meaning is influenced by social and cultural factors. It includes the study of speech acts, such as requests, apologies, and compliments, and the role of context in interpreting meaning. It involves the analysis of the social, cultural, and situational context in which language is used, as well as the intentions and goals of the speakers and listeners. Pragmatics plays an important role in language structure, as it allows speakers to use language effectively in different social and cultural contexts.

Pragmatics helps both speakers and listeners to understand the implicit meanings of words and expressions and to use language in a way that is appropriate to the social and cultural norms of their community. To undertake successful politeness, for instance, we need to be deeply familiar with the set of pragmatics in a culture. Politeness norms vary across cultures, and pragmatics helps individuals navigate these norms to express their cultural identity. For instance, in some cultures, using honorifics or titles to address someone of higher social status is important, while in others, a more informal and egalitarian approach is preferred. In certain cultures, it may be common to express disagreement indirectly or to use euphemisms to address sensitive topics. Adhering to these cultural preferences allows individuals to convey their cultural identity effectively.

> Societal pragmatics and intercultural pragmatics have to be seen as interconnected; even though intercultural pragmatics, with its emphasis on "emergent" norms of interaction may seem to represent a tendency towards autonomy. . . . We believe that pragmemes are indexed to the culture in which they are immersed; whereas in some cases, pragmatic principles are modularized-an apparent violation of Occam's (modified) razor, which compels us to avoid unnecessary entities, including unnecessary principles.
>
> (Capone & Mey, 2015, p. 5)

Pragmatics enables individuals to utilise non-verbal cues to express their cultural identity. For instance, hand gestures that are commonly used in a specific culture, or maintaining eye contact during conversations, can be important markers of cultural identity. Pragmatics can also be used to create new expressions and idioms that reflect cultural identity. In some cultures, there may be expressions or idioms that are based on the social and cultural context in which they are used.

Morphology

In linguistics, morphology refers to the mental system involved in word formation or to the branch of linguistics that deals with words and their internal structure. Morphologists investigate how words are formed and analyse their inner construction. "A morpheme may consist of a word, such as hand, or a meaningful piece of a word, such as the –ed of looked, that cannot be divided into smaller meaningful parts" (Aronoff & Fudeman, 2011, p. 2). One thing that makes a morpheme a morpheme is that it recurs, and thus speakers are able to identify it and give it meaning. When two or more instances of a given morpheme occur with different shapes, we call them allomorphs (Aronoff & Fudeman, 2011, pp. 2 and 15).

Morphology plays an important role in language structure, as it allows speakers to create new words and change the meaning of existing words by adding, removing, or changing morphemes.

> It may be useful to mention that when we change the order of words in a sentence, we generally also change the meaning. When we change the order of morphemes in a word, we generally end up with something ungrammatical.
>
> (Aronoff & Fudeman, 2011, p. 38)

Morphology can also play a role in cultural identity. The way that words are formed and the meanings that they convey can reflect cultural values, beliefs, and practices. For example, in many cultures, there are words that are used to describe complex social relationships or emotions that may not exist in other cultures. These words can reflect the importance of such relationships or emotions in that culture.

Morphology can also be used to create new words and expressions that reflect cultural identity. For example, in English, words such as "selfie" and "hashtag" were created through the combination of existing morphemes to reflect new cultural phenomena. Mark Aronoff and Kirsten Fudeman (2011, p. 4) report an interesting case of creating a new word in New York:

> If you had been walking down the street in Ithaca, New York, a few years ago, you might have looked up and seen a sign for the music store "Rebop," a name that owes its inspiration to the jazz term *rebop*. *Rebop* was originally one of the many nonsense expressions that jazz musicians

> threw into their vocal improvisations, starting in the early 1920s. In the 1940s, *rebop* became interchangeable with *bebop*, a term of similar origin, as the term for the rhythmically and harmonically eccentric music played by young black musicians. By the 1950s the name of this musical style was quite firmly established as simply *bop*. Today, the original use of *rebop* is known only to cognoscenti, so that most people who pass by the store will be likely to interpret the word as composed of the word *bop* and the prefix *re-*, which means approximately "again." This prefix can attach only to verbs, so we must interpret *bop* as a verb here. *Rebop* must therefore mean "bop again," if it means anything at all. And this music store, appropriately, specialized in selling used CDs. There's something going on here with English morphology. Of course, *rebop* is not a perfectly well-formed English word. The verb *bop* means something like "bounce," but the prefix *re-*normally attaches only to a verb whose meaning denotes an accomplishment. The verb *rebop* therefore makes little sense. But names of stores and products are designed to catch the consumer's attention, not necessarily to make sense, and this one does so by exploiting people's knowledge of English in a fairly complex way and breaking the rules so as to attract attention, as verbal art often does.

In most cultures, there are strict rules for the formation of words, such as the use of gendered nouns or the use of honorifics. The use of morphology in audio design not only enriches gameplay but also preserves and celebrates cultural practices, delivering an authentic experience for players on multiple levels. Much like the whimsical creation of names such as "Rebop," which blends cultural references with morphological innovation, video game audio can playfully subvert traditional linguistic rules to amplify players' cultural experiences.

Rhythm in Language

Another aspect of language is its rhythm. "Stress-timed" and "syllable-timed" are used to characterise the pronunciation of languages that display a particular type of rhythm. In stress-timed languages like English, there is a tendency that stressed syllables to recur at regular intervals, regardless of the number of unstressed syllables that intervene in a sentence. In other words, the amount of time it takes to say a sentence in stress-timed language depends on the number of syllables that receive stress, either minor or major, not on the total number of syllables (Avery & Ehrlich, 1992). In syllable-timed languages like Persian, on the other hand, the syllables are said to occur at regular intervals of time, and the amount of time it takes to say a sentence depends on the number of syllables in the sentence, not on the number of stressed syllables as in stress-timed languages (Ohata, 2004, p. 9). First, we will have a brief review on the rhythm in language and music.

Musical rhythm is an organisation of sound events along the line of time accessible to the auditory senses. There are similarities between rhythm in speech and music, one of them is grouping structure. In speech, the words of a sentence are not perceived as being equally separated from one another. Rather the boundaries between words vary in the amount of perceived juncture so that some words group together to form larger rhythmic chunks or phrases. A similar situation occurs in music, where the tones of a melodic line are usually perceived as being organised into phrases even if there is no physical discontinuity between tones. Some of the acoustic cues to phrase boundaries in language and music, such as pitch drop and durational lengthening, are similar (Ohata, 2004, p. 9).

Rhythm in speech is a composite of several aspects of a language that influence how it is organised in time based on the following issues and factors. Here we briefly review salient similarities and differences between speech rhythm and musical rhythm based on the category presented by Aniruddh D. Patel (2003, p. 140):

- The first issue is the pattern of grouping/phrasing of words within utterances and pausing between utterances. For instance, in a duologue among a game characters, the rhythm may be structured to create anticipation: "You can achieve a high score . . . if you believe in yourself." (The pause after "score" allows the audience to reflect and engage before the punch line.)
- The second factor is the durational patterning of syllables which is crucially important in syllable-timed languages. For instance, consider the phrase "J'aime le chocolat" (I love chocolate) in French as a syllable-timed language, each syllable in this sentence is pronounced with a similar length, and the timing between the syllables is consistent.
- The third factor is the configurational patterning of stressed versus unstressed syllables. For example, English has a roughly alternating pattern of stressed and unstressed syllables and has mechanisms to avoid too many stressed syllables in close adjacency (stress clashes) or long sequences of unstressed syllables (stress lapses). Greek, in contrast, has a greater tolerance for stress lapses, so stressed syllables do not recur as regularly as they do in English.

There is a popular idea in musicology that claims the linguist rhythm of a culture might have an imprint impact on its musical rhythm. Patel and Daniele (2003) researched this issue and focused on cultures with strong linguistic rhythmic differences and compared the musical rhythms of these cultures using the same measures that had been applied to speech rhythm. The normalised pairwise variability index (nPVI) permitted them to accomplish this task by evaluating the relative variability within a collection of durations, applicable to event durations in various forms such as vowels in language and musical tones in music. They particularly focused on the speech and music of England and France, because English and French are canonical examples of languages with different rhythms. They applied the nPVI to the musical themes of 16 composers (six English and ten French) and found that on average, English and French musical themes had significantly different nPVI values. This investigation demonstrated that English had a greater variability of vowel duration. In this investigation, the focus was exclusively on instrumental music in order to examine the rhythmic thinking of composers when they were free of a linguistic context. Their data suggest that even when thinking instrumentally, composers can be influenced by the rhythms of their native language (to read more on this research look at Patel & Daniele, 2003).

Tempo of Speech

The tempo of speech is determined by the rate at which words are spoken and the length of pauses between sentences or phrases. The tempo of speech can be influenced by factors such as language proficiency, emotion, and cultural background. Changes in tempo reflects emotions such as excitement or anger, physical wellbeing, or energy level. Jason S. Wrench and his colleagues (2020, p. 163) report that "One of the author's aunts is a brittle diabetic. When talking to her aunt, the author can detect whether the aunt's blood sugar is too low if her aunt is speaking extremely slow."

In addition to personal and emotional factors, the ways in which individuals articulate their thoughts can reveal much about their cultural backgrounds. Speech tempo can illustrate cultural identity, as it often reflects the communication styles and social norms of different communities. Edgar's (2019) exploration of the intersection between musical notation and the spoken voice highlights the significance of cultural influences on speech tempo, suggesting that interdisciplinary studies can enrich our understanding of this relationship. By emphasising the potential connections between musical elements and dialectical characteristics, Edgar echoes Philip Tagg's (2011) assertion regarding the reciprocal nature of influence between music and spoken language. This framework invites further research into how contemporary musical trends might shape speech patterns, particularly in popular culture, ultimately fostering sonic literacy that resonates with broader audiences.

Understanding the role of culture in shaping speech tempo deepens our appreciation of the nuances in human communication. Certain cultures may have a preference for speaking at a faster pace, while in others, they may speak more slowly. For example, in industrial cultures such as America or Japan where the overall tempo of life is fast and time is highly important speech tends to be fast-paced to emphasise efficiency and productivity. In contrast, in some Latin American or Middle Eastern cultures, people may speak at a slower pace, focusing more on building relationships and maintaining social connections. In some cultures, where directness is highly valued, people may speak more quickly to convey information efficiently. In contrast, in cultures that prioritise indirect communication, speech may be slower as more context and non-verbal cues are provided to convey meaning. In addition, in cultures that value politeness and respect for turn-taking, people may speak more slowly, ensuring everyone has a chance to contribute. Non-verbal gestures also influence the tempo of speech. Animated non-verbal cues, such as hand gestures, facial expressions, or body movements may lead to a perception of faster speech when they are used alongside spoken words.

By linking these cultural insights to modern applications, we can better understand how speech tempo enhances narrative experiences in various media. For example, a character involved in a deep conversation or experiencing distress might deliver their lines at a slower pace, in keeping with culturally specific speech patterns. This intentional pacing allows for reflective pauses that highlight their internal struggle.

Intensity of Speech

The intensity of speech, encompassing aspects such as volume and energy, not only reflects individual emotions but also varies significantly across different cultural and social contexts. When individuals speak loudly, the increased volume may be used to convey anger, emotional distress, happiness, or heightened excitement. When they speak at a lower volume, the decreased volume may be an effort to diffuse an emotionally intense conversation. People often lower their voices when they are in close proximity to someone, such as whispering in their ear or speaking intimately in a romantic setting. Speaking softly can also be a sign of respect or politeness.

The intensity of speech is also influenced by everyday life in particular regions, where the dynamics of social interaction shape how inhabitants express themselves. For instance, in communities where social interactions are frequent and lively, such as in bustling urban environments or at festive gatherings, individuals may adopt a higher intensity of speech as a means of capturing attention and conveying enthusiasm. The excitement of local markets or communal celebrations encourages louder voices and animated exchanges, reinforcing the idea that passion and engagement are celebrated. Conversely, in quieter, rural settings where conversation often occurs in more intimate contexts – like during family meals or small gatherings – individuals may favour a softer approach, prioritising restraint and consideration for their listeners. This cultural norm promotes connection and understanding over the more boisterous exchanges seen in larger communities.

Cultural perceptions of speech intensity vary as well. In some cultures, a high intensity of speech may be seen as a sign of passion, enthusiasm, or assertiveness. People may speak loudly, use expressive gestures, and show strong emotions during conversations. This level of intensity is often seen as normal and engaging. In other cultures, a low intensity of speech may be preferred or considered more appropriate. People may speak softly, use subtle gestures, and maintain a calm demeanour during conversations. This lower intensity is often valued for its perceived politeness, respect, and modesty. For instance, in Indian culture, a high intensity of speech is common, particularly in animated discussions or debates; while a low intensity may be perceived as a lack of interest or engagement. However, in Japanese culture, a moderate intensity of speech is preferred, with extremes of high or low intensity considered impolite or disrespectful.

While cultural perceptions of speech intensity influence conversational styles around the world, recent linguistic studies reveal that environmental factors, particularly temperature, also play a critical role in shaping the phonetic characteristics and intensity of speech in different regions. A research by Wang and his colleagues (2023) indicates that languages spoken in colder regions tend to exhibit a higher prevalence of consonants and more complex consonant clusters compared to those in warmer climates, where vowels are more abundant and sonority is generally higher. For example, Russian and Georgian languages, found in colder zones, often include intricate consonant combinations that are less common in the vowel-rich speech of tropical languages, such as Hawaiian or Edo. The relationship can be attributed to the acoustic effects of temperature on sound transmission; warmer air absorbs high-frequency sound components, which adversely affects the clarity of consonant sounds. This results in a preference for sonorous sounds that can resist attenuation in warmer climates. Furthermore, the influence of temperature on speech patterns extends beyond mere phonetic variations, intersecting with broader socio-ecological factors, such as population density and communal activities, underscoring the intricate interplay between environmental conditions and linguistic evolution in shaping diverse phonetic systems across cultures.

Language and Localisation Strategies

Localisation goes beyond simply transferring the linguistic assets of the software product. It requires much more than "text-to-text translation" and must take into consideration the sociocultural, religious characteristics of the target market and accordingly adapt the game to the target culture. These processes also include matching the layout, text orientation, and language script requirements and conventions to those of the target language. Video game localisation not only involves the translation of in-game texts but also includes language encoding, text orientation, texts on images, subtitling, and dubbing (Jiménez-Crespo, 2013 and 2019; Bernal-Merino, 2020; Al-Batineh & Alawneh, 2021).

British and Americans both speak English, but their cultural background may lead to different interpretations of what they say.

> If we were talking and I said, "it's time for tea," you may think that I'm going to put on some boiling water and pull out the oolong tea. However, if I said, "it's time for tea" in the United Kingdom, you would assume that we were getting ready for our evening meal. Same word, but two very different meanings depending on the culture one uses the term.
>
> (Wrench et al., 2020)

While the creativity and imagination of the translator are necessary to guarantee the game keeps the user entertained in the process of game localisation, functionality first takes place in the software localisation paradigm (Onar & Çatak, 2022, p. 94). Unfortunately, not everyone who can write can also translate, and not everyone who can translate can write. While video game localisation includes a wide range of activities and specialists, the main activity is communication via language translation, and it is important to realise that the connection between these two processes is complex (Pym, 2004). William Gibbons (2021, p. 359) believes "developers often deliberately eliminate or minimise region-specific identifiers through a process called localisation, in which aspects of a game are adapted to fit the perceived cultural norms and preferences of a target market."

The difference between translation and localisation is a confusing issue. Localisation is defined as the process of altering a product, a game, or a piece of software while taking cultural and linguistic differences into account to make the content more appropriate for the target culture and audience. Along with translation, the process of localisation involves several issues most of which appeared in the current volume, whereas translation is the process of converting a text from one language to another while preserving the text's meaning in both languages. The translatable variables adhere to their syntactic type, gender, and number, and may cause major issues when a game is localised into a language with a quite different syntactic and morphological system. Some languages are synthetic, that is, languages that depend on inflections to build and express syntactic relations and in such cases, the grammatical gender and number of the variable should be matched with other grammatical elements in the string to avoid awkward translations (Al-Batineh & Alawneh, 2021, p. 47–8).

Video games sometimes are full of jokes designed to entertain and please the player; therefore, humour is a crucial component. Wordplay, linguistic anomalies, and puns are all used to create a variety of amusing jokes, many of which cannot be translated directly since they are derived from culturally established colloquial language. They must be culturally and linguistically appropriate for the target language and culture, or else meaning is lost, and adapting is necessary to compensate for the loss of humour, even if this requires significant changes to the original work. If there is a partial or complete loss of meaning during translation, translators may resort to partial rewriting to produce functional counterparts (Di Marco, 2007, p. 6).

In almost all languages, speaking may not necessarily be in accordance with writing. We will focus on the Arabic language as our case study in this discussion. When localising a video game for an Arabic audience, it is crucial to consider the distinctive features of the Arabic language in both its written and spoken forms, as these can vary significantly from one another. The writing issues include text orientation, cursive script, and encoding (see Al-Batineh, 2021, pp. 51–60). In Arabic, the tone of certain vocal commentators may not align consistently with specific characters, and you may realise that one of the lines does not fit properly in a certain context, although it is linguistically correct (Mendoza, 2021). Another spoken issue in the Arabic language is that speakers prefer to select words and sentences that contain minimum letters and words. This is why despite the matchless eloquence, smoothness and flow, Arabic looks relatively shorter than other languages (Madani, 2020, p. 31).

The next issue to consider is the articulators. The human voice is capable of producing numerous sounds, but language articulations generally are categorised into the group of six based on the organ that plays the main role in producing the sound, including "throat," "palate," "tongue," "gums," "teeth" and "lips." Arabs benefit from nearly all of them in their spoken language.

Saying "Hi!" in English takes less than a second, while the equivalent greeting, "Marhaba," in Arabic, takes about three times longer. This presents a significant challenge when converting dialogues and subtitles between languages, especially in terms of fitting them within the required time and space constraints. Additionally, written English is often more formal than spoken English, a trend that can be observed in other languages as well.

Dubbing is essential for reaching a broader audience that seeks a complete and immersive gaming experience. Challenges of dubbing can be summarised in three main issues including culture, aesthetics, and lip-sync.

- Culture can be said to be a main challenge in the *audio* part of the audiovisual industry. It is essential to ensure that the dubbing maintains the original intent and meaning, while also resonating with the target audience's cultural context. Although language is an essential but imperfect representation of culture, culture also plays a major role in text comprehension. The translators' duty is therefore not just to convey an information structure; they must also mediate across various cultural components by relying on common human experience (Newmark, 1991, pp. 74 and 131).

  Every culture has some sensitive topics that could affect how the target audience receives the localised product. For Arabic audiences, for instance, we should be careful in the course of localisation about things like alcohol, religious symbols or mentioning verses from the Quran or the Bible, homosexuality, explicit sexual scenes, and so on. In such situations, translators make some amendments to the translated version in a way that will not culturally offend Arab gamers (Abdo, 2022). This challenge requires skilled translators and adaptation experts who can strike a balance between faithfulness to the source material and cultural relevance. This is because any gap between two different cultures which is not or cannot be bridged may cause alienation between the audience and the characters. Moreover, this may also result in the fact that the audience will listen to impersonating characters (actors speaking the target language), who are well known, speaking a dialogue (source text) that does not belong to their culture.

- The issue of aesthetics in dubbing is particularly important and contributes to the success or failure of a dubbed audiovisual material. The goal is to create a seamless audiovisual experience for the audience. This means that the dialogue needs to be synchronised with the characters' lip movements, body language, and overall timing. This is because dubbing creates a kind of interaction between the viewers and the impersonating voices, especially if the viewers are familiar with these voices. As a result, if the actions and words contradict the image that the viewers have drawn in their minds about those characters, then a barrier between the viewers and the audiovisual material may result. Skilled voice actors and meticulous editing are crucial to ensure that the dubbing aligns perfectly with the on-screen actions.
- Lip-sync is another significant challenge in dubbing. The movement of the characters' lips in the original language needs to match the dubbed dialogue as closely as possible. This requires careful attention to detail and accurate timing to ensure a natural and believable lip-sync experience. Fodor (1976, p. 9) sets three requirements for dubbing to be successful. These are related to content, lip (phonetic) synchrony, and character synchrony:

  - Content synchrony can be said to be related to a good translation or writing of the script into the target language. Its importance results from the fact that the target text will be the major element in determining the success of audiovisuals. The reason is that some violations in lip synchronisation and character synchrony can be tolerated, but content that does not speak to the target text audience or which is grossly violated (changed to suit the target culture) is not acceptable.
  - As far as phonetic synchrony is concerned, Fodor (1976, p. 21) defines it as the visible sound formation in the picture and the purport of the source text which are the decisive factors in shaping the target sounds and their sequences in correct speech. Many games use the lip-sync technique and others do not, but in the video games which use this technique, the dubbing process must be done carefully in order to create an immersive environment for the player. Due to our purpose in this book which is examining cultural issues not dubbing techniques in video games, we will not investigate lip synchronisation issues.

- Character synchrony in dubbing means the harmony between the performing characters and the dubbing voices of the characters in terms of temper, reaction, body movement, and language. Characters in video games often have a wide range of personality traits, with distinct expressions, regional speech patterns, and mannerisms that enhance the portrayal of their characters and differentiate them from one another (Onar & Çatak, 2022, p. 96). To put it differently, if there is a contradiction between what we see and what we hear, then a kind of discomfort will result. One example of this is when a young character is dubbed by an older one or when an evil character is dubbed by a romantic one. Fodor (1976) describes this technique as a psychological aspect of dubbing and stresses that it is essential for there to be a correspondence between the source and target sounds if the voice of the dubbing actor does not match the personality and deportment of the visible character, then character diachrony is likely to occur. Character synchrony and the extent of cultural differences contribute to the success or failure of a dubbed material (Alkadi, 2010, pp. 48–65).

It is worth noting that the dialogue between characters is written in a colloquial style. The translators working on localisation must pay close attention to this to ensure that the original text's meaning is preserved. Even if a completely different technique is employed, the basic meaning of the source text must be maintained for the target text to be properly adapted. The ages of the characters are also important; a child may speak differently than an adult in most instances, and an old person may repeat words common from earlier generations. There are no straightforward solutions when it comes to localisation; the goal is to preserve the gaming experience, and it is critical to understand the game's history, previous games or editions from the series, cultural references, historical elements, or any other relevant media counterparts (Onar & Çatak, 2022, p. 100). Overcoming the challenges of dubbing discussed above requires a collaborative effort from linguists, translators, voice actors, audio engineers, and other professionals involved in the dubbing process. With the right expertise and creativity, they can work together to deliver a high-quality dubbed version that successfully captures the essence of the original content while appealing to the target audience.

Chapter 4

Non-verbal Speech Sounds and Expressing Emotions

Introduction

While language is a crucial part of human communication, it is incapable of capturing the full depth and nuance of human communication and has limitations in delivering a considerable part of human senses and emotions. Non-verbal expressions in many ways complement, accent, or even substitute for the use of words. In general, all aspects of communication other than the use of words are referred to as "non-verbal" communication. It contains a wide range of behaviours and cues, including facial, eye contact, posture and gestures, tone of voice, physical proximity, touching, appearance, silence, etc.

Edward Hall (1959) brings a smart outlook of Sherlock Holmes as an example to emphasise the place of non-verbal importance in communication. He says Sir Arthur Conan Doyle's success with his creation, Sherlock Holmes, is largely attributable to the fact that Holmes knew how to make the most of non-verbal communication and extracted the maximum from what he observed. The following excerpt from "A Case of Identity" aptly illustrates this point.

> He had risen from his chair and was standing between the parted blinds, gazing down into the dull neutral-tinted London street. Looking over his shoulder, I saw that on the pavement opposite there stood a large woman with a heavy fur boa around her neck, and a large curling red feather in a broad-brimmed hat which was tilted in a coquettish Duchess of Devonshire fashion over her ear. From under this great panoply she peeped up in a nervous, hesitating fashion at our windows, while her body oscillated backward and forward, and her fingers fidgeted with her glove buttons. Suddenly, with a plunge, as of the swimmer who leaves the bank, she hurried across the road and we heard the sharp clang of the bell.
>
> "I have seen those symptoms before," said Holmes, throwing his cigarette into the fire. "Oscillation upon the pavement always means an *affaire de coeur.*[1] She would like advice but is not sure that the matter is not too delicate for communication. And yet even here we may discriminate.

DOI: 10.4324/9781003591399-5

> When a woman has been seriously wronged by a man she no longer oscillates, and the usual symptom is a broken bell wire. Here we may take it that there is a love matter, but that the maiden is not so much angry as perplexed, or grieved. But here she comes in person to resolve our doubts."
>
> (Hall, 1959, pp. 57–58)

Hall believes that Sir Arthur made explicit a highly complex process that many of us go through without knowing that we are involved. Those of us who keep our eyes open can read volumes into what we see going on around us. The principles highlighted by Edward Hall regarding non-verbal communication are applicable in video games in various ways. Just as Sherlock Holmes adeptly interprets the subtle cues of human behaviour to unravel complex situations, game developers can leverage sound design to convey emotions, character intentions, and narrative depth without the need for explicit dialogue. As players navigate through richly designed worlds, they can become attuned to the non-verbal cues embedded in audio – deciphering tensions, foreshadowing events, and understanding character dynamics, thereby enriching their engagement and connection with the game. In this way, the world of video game audio becomes a silent yet powerful communicator, resonating with Hall's assertion that keen observation can reveal deeper truths hidden in plain sight.

Indeed, the majority of video games prioritise clear, unambiguous communication, especially when conveying essential gameplay information. Players are often tasked with rapidly processing objectives, navigating complex environments, and executing precise actions. For instance, in a fast-paced action game, players need to instantly understand where to go and what enemies to engage, leaving little room for deciphering subtle audio cues. Therefore, developers frequently employ direct dialogue, visual cues like glowing objectives or directional arrows, and on-screen prompts such as health bars and button instructions to ensure clarity and avoid player frustration.

While certain genres, such as investigative or stealth games like *L.A. Noire* or *Metal Gear Solid*, might leverage subtle audio cues – a distant footstep, a hushed whisper – to enhance immersion and realism, the practical application of solely relying on these cues faces significant limitations in the information-dense environment of most games. The challenge arises from the inherent need for players to quickly process and react to dynamic information. Imagine a real-time strategy game where players must simultaneously manage resources and command units; subtle audio cues alone would be inadequate to convey the urgency of an incoming attack.

While the potential of sound design to convey atmosphere and character emotion is undeniable, relying solely on it to deliver critical gameplay information risks player confusion and frustration. Even meticulously crafted audio cues, like a change in music tempo or a specific sound effect, can be easily missed or misinterpreted amidst the cacophony of in-game stimuli.

Consequently, developers often prioritise explicit communication through visual indicators, on-screen text, and direct dialogue to ensure reliable information delivery. For example, a flashing icon on the screen can indicate a low health warning far more effectively than a subtle change in the character's breathing. Ultimately, effective game design necessitates a balance between the artistic potential of sound design for atmospheric depth and the functional imperative of clear, robust communication.

Biological and Cultural Factors

Humans have species-typical vocalisations, but men vocalisations are often overshadowed by a diverse range of culturally learned non-linguistic vocalisations. "Only the most salient and involuntary vocalizations remain universal and distinct enough to be perceived categorically in all cultures, with laughter being the paradigmatic example" (Anikin et al., 2018, p. 58). Biological factors refer to the innate or genetic aspects of emotions, such as physiological responses and brain structures involved in emotional processing. On the other hand, cultural factors encompass the socially learned and shared expectations, norms, and values that shape our emotional experiences. While it is widely accepted that both biological and cultural factors play roles in the emotion process, there is still much to be understood about the specific extent to which each factor contributes. The studies of Mesquita, Frijda, and Scherer highlighted the need for further exploration into the relative contributions of these factors and the amount of variance they explain (see Scherer, 1979). Determining the respective contributions of biological and cultural factors can be a complex task, as they often interact and influence each other. For instance, cultural norms can regulate the expression and experience of certain emotions, which in turn affects physiological responses. Likewise, biological factors can influence the development and expression of emotions within specific cultural contexts.

The interplay between biological and cultural factors in emotional expression is vital for communicating with a massive audience in new media, such as video games. We can leverage insights from vocalisation studies by crafting sound elements that resonate with universal emotional cues, such as laughter or gasps, while also integrating culturally specific auditory elements that reflect the game's setting and narrative. This approach creates an emotional landscape that acknowledges the biological underpinnings of human reactions while simultaneously respecting and incorporating cultural contexts.

The Two Means of Non-verbal Communications

In this chapter we focus on two streams of non-verbal communication: non-linguistic vocalisations and non-verbal emotions. Although both are considered important means of non-verbal communication, there are some differences between them in origin, usage, complexity, purpose, specificity, development, and control.

Non-linguistic vocalisations seem to have an innate, biological basis while non-verbal expressions of emotions are largely learned through culture and experience. Concerning complexity, we can say that non-linguistic vocalisations tend to be holistic sounds conveying a global emotional state. While, non-verbal expressions of emotions can be more nuanced and multipart, combining different facial expressions, gestures, and postures. Non-linguistic vocalisations are used in a more primal communicative function, especially in contexts of danger, distress, or arousal but non-verbal expressions are used in social connections and interactions.

The ability to produce non-linguistic vocalisations presents from our birth while non-verbal expression of emotions develops and becomes more nuanced with our age and experience within the society we develop in. From birth, humans possess an innate ability to produce non-linguistic vocalisations, such as crying and cooing, which serve as fundamental means of communication and emotional expression. These early vocalisations are critical for survival, as they signal needs and feelings to caregivers. As individuals grow and engage with their environment, the non-verbal expression of emotions becomes increasingly sophisticated, influenced by cultural norms, social interactions, and personal experiences. This progression involves the refinement of vocal qualities – such as pitch, tone, and rhythm – alongside the integration of non-verbal cues like facial expressions and body language. For instance, a toddler's simple shrieks may evolve into vocalisations that convey joy, frustration, or distress, reflecting both the maturation of their vocal apparatus and their growing understanding of social contexts.

The degree of our control of different non-verbal expressions is different. We have limited control over non-linguistic vocalisations, particularly at times of danger, excitement, sadness, etc., compared to our emotional expressions. These vocalisations are deeply rooted in our evolutionary biology, serving as immediate indicators of emotional states that may elicit responses from others in our environment, often occurring outside of conscious awareness or intention. In contrast, our emotional expressions – such as facial expressions, body language, and gestures – tend to be more modifiable and can be consciously regulated to a greater extent.

Non-linguistic Vocalisations

Non-linguistic vocalisations refer to vocal sounds that are not words or speech, yet can convey semantical or sensational messages. Non-verbal sounds are a wide range of vocal expressions that reflect a person's emotional state, physical condition, or reaction to situations, without using actual words. As pointed out earlier, non-linguistic vocalisations seem to have an innate, biological basis that has been with us since our birth. However, the way they are used in different contexts may vary from one culture to another. Non-linguistic vocalisations mostly tend to convey general affective states like pleasure, pain, arousal, etc. For instance, vocalisations conveying anger likely occur universally in all languages and cultures, but particular acoustic manifestations of anger could vary as a function of many linguistic and articulatory production factors, as well as pragmatic rules (Mesquita & Frijda, 1992, p. 179).

Recognition accuracy of general non-linguistic vocalisation in cross-cultural studies demonstrates that non-linguistic sounds have some culture-specific component (Anikin et al., 2018, p. 55). A great deal of our communications in private and social connections occur through non-verbal means. Some examples of common non-verbal speech sounds are

- Laughing: conveying joy, amusement, or sometimes embarrassment
- Crying: conveying a natural emotional response, like sadness, pain, or distress
- Screaming/Yelling: expressing anger, frustration, fear, excitement, or alarm
- Grunting/Groaning: indicating effort or physical exertion
- Sighing: showing boredom, frustration, sadness, or tiredness
- Gasping: expressing surprise, shock, or horror
- Moaning: suggesting pleasure, pain, physical discomfort, dissatisfaction, or longing
- Giggling: expressing a quiet or restrained form of laughter, often to cover up nervousness
- Snoring: happening when the airways vibrate during sleep, usually an involuntary sound
- Sniffling: often accompanying crying or having discomfort, illness, or runny nose
- Coughing: indicating discomfort, illness, or trying to get attention
- Yawning: indicating tiredness or boredom
- Throat clearing: expressing discomfort or trying to get attention
- Clicking: expressing disappointment or annoyance
- Hisses: expressing annoyance, anger, or urging silence
- Gasps: expressing surprise, shock, or alarm
- Whistling: expressing surprise, impressment, or getting attention
- Humming: expressing contentment, happiness, or thinking

When people lack common words to convey their meaning, they can improvise iconic gestures to ground communication about varied domains like actions, shape and size, and spatial relationships. "This remarkable human ability is the foundation of the parlor game 'charades,' and it is thought to play an important role in language acquisition and evolution" (Ćwiek et al., 2021, p. 1). Unlike gestures which can visually depict ideas, it was believed that the auditory modality does not lend itself well to visually representing various concepts beyond sound. Nonetheless, there is growing evidence that iconic vocalisations can convey a much wider range of meanings than previously supposed.

> Cross-linguistic research also documents the widespread occurrence of ideophones (also called mimetics or expressive), a distinct class of depictive words used to express vivid meanings in semantic domains like sound (i.e., onomatopoeia), manner of motion, size, visual patterns, textures, and even inner feelings and cognitive states.
>
> (Ćwiek et al., 2021, p. 3)

Listeners can extract more information from vocalisations produced by members of the same cultural group, indicating that there is important cultural variation in human non-linguistic vocalisations (Anikin et al., 2018, p. 58). Aleksandra Ćwiek and her colleagues (2021) reported the results of an extensive cross-cultural study to test whether people from different cultural and linguistic backgrounds are able to infer the meanings of the vocalisations with similarly high levels of accuracy. Their study indicated the possibility that iconic vocalisations could have supported the emergence of an open-ended symbolic system. While this undercuts a principal argument in favour of the primary role of gestures in the origins of language, it raises the question of how vocalisations would compare to gestures in a cross-cultural test. Laboratory experiments in which English-speaking participants played charades-like communication games have shown better performance with gestures than with non-linguistic vocalisations, although vocalisations are still effective to a significant extent. They conclude that both modalities, visual and auditory, could work together in tandem, each better suited for communicating under different environmental conditions (e.g., daylight vs. darkness), social contexts (e.g., whether the audience is positioned to better see or hear the signal), and the meaning to be expressed (e.g., animals, actions, emotions, abstractions).

Human language, unlike animal vocalisations, is both versatile and potent for communication. It relies on a culture-specific code passed down socially, meaning we are not naturally born speaking a particular language like German or Persian. However,

> there is mounting evidence that non-linguistic sounds such as laughter are more similar to the vocalizations of other mammals than they are to human language. This evidence comes from neurological research on vocal production and psychological research on vocal perception.
>
> (Anikin et al., 2018, p. 54)

The power of non-linguistic vocalisations not only bridges the gap between gameplay and emotional response but also underscores the potential of sound design as a vital component of interactive storytelling in video games. Game designers can harness culture-specific aspects of these vocalisations to create immersive environments that resonate with players from diverse backgrounds, allowing them to interpret emotional contexts without requiring linguistic clarity. Furthermore, as players navigate various scenarios, iconic vocalisations can serve as intuitive signals, guiding them through gameplay mechanics or heightening the impact of narrative moments. The integration of auditory and visual cues crafts a multifaceted communication system that mirrors the complexity of human interactions, thereby enriching the storytelling and emotional depth of the games.

Non-verbal Emotions

Common non-verbal emotions include amusement, anger, awe, confusion, contempt, contentment, desire, disappointment, disgust, distress, ecstasy, elation, embarrassment, fear, interest, pain, realisation, relief, sadness, surprise (positive), surprise (negative), sympathy, and triumph.

While we have words for many emotions, non-verbal sounds provide a quicker, more visceral way to communicate and connect with others. They tend to be spontaneous, instinctual responses that carry meaning on a subconscious level. In a study, the ability of non-verbal vocal expressions to convey a range of emotions across different cultures was explored by Laukka et al. (2013). By analysing vocalisations from actors representing diverse backgrounds (India, Kenya, Singapore, and the USA), the researchers found that listeners from Sweden could reliably recognise multiple emotions from these vocalisations, achieving accuracy levels above chance for both positive and negative emotions. Notably, emotions such as relief, anger, and disgust were easily identified, while self-conscious emotions like pride and guilt showed lower recognition rates, indicating potential cultural and cognitive complexities in their expression. The findings support the notion that vocalisations serve as a universal medium for conveying emotional states, providing valuable insights into the nature of non-verbal communication and its implications in emotional science. Overall, this work underlines the importance of exploring various emotional modalities beyond the conventional focus on basic emotions and highlights the potential for non-linguistic vocalisations to enhance understanding of cross-cultural emotional communication.

In another study, Itziar Fernández and colleagues (2000) explore how cultural dimensions significantly influence emotional expression across various societies. It emphasises the complexities in understanding culture, noting that simplistic definitions equating culture with country may overlook important intra-country variations. The findings indicate that women generally exhibit more emotional expressiveness than men, although this gender difference is less pronounced in Asian cultures due to rigid normative display rules. Notably, the study highlights that countries with high human development indices tend to have more intense emotional expressions, reinforcing the idea that socio-economic factors are intertwined with cultural norms.

Non-verbal speech sounds serve as important emotional cues in human interactions. Nonetheless, some non-verbal sounds are commonly used in specific cultures:

- Tutting: In some European cultures like the UK, tutting is a sound made by clicking the tongue against the roof of the mouth to express disapproval or irritation.
- Um-hum: In the southern US, making a humming sound while nodding is used to show agreement or acknowledgement, more so than just saying "yes."
- Clucking: In some African cultures, making a tongue click sound is used to get someone's attention or express disapproval.
- Shushing: The "shh" sound is used more commonly in some Asian cultures to signal someone to be quiet.
- Huffing: In Hispanic cultures, huffing or puffing out air loudly through the mouth can communicate annoyance or exasperation.
- Snapping: Finger snapping is used as a call or signal in some parts of Africa and the Middle East.
- Whistling: Whistling is used to call or signal someone in various cultures all over the world, especially in rural areas.
- Smacking lips: In some West African cultures, smacking the lips softly is used to show appreciation for food.

There are also regional variations in the use and meanings of common non-verbal sounds across cultures. For example, sighing may express relief in one culture but annoyance in another.

The important thing to note is that for effective cross-cultural communication, it's helpful to be aware of differences in the use of non-verbal sounds and avoid making judgements based solely on your own cultural interpretations. Listening carefully and seeking clarification can help avoid misunderstandings.

Petri Laukka and his colleagues (2013) conducted an experiment in which actors from India, Kenya, Singapore, and the USA were instructed to produce vocalisations that would convey nine positive and nine negative emotions to listeners. The vocalisations were judged by Swedish listeners using a within-valence forced-choice procedure, where positive and negative emotions were judged in separate experiments. The results of this research showed that the voice can reveal both basic emotions and several positive emotions other than happiness across cultures, but self-conscious emotions such as guilt, pride, and shame seem not to be well recognised from non-linguistic vocalisations and have to be interpreted based on the cultural norms.

A certain non-verbal sound may have an entirely different meaning in different cultures. A good example is the sound of clicking the tongue, which has very different meanings in different cultures:

- In some African cultures, clicking the tongue is a common way to call or get someone's attention, show disapproval, or convey other emotions. It's a natural part of communication.
- In Western cultures like the US and Europe, tongue-clicking is often seen as rude or impolite. It can convey impatience, annoyance, or disapproval.
- In some Asian cultures, tongue-clicking is generally avoided and not commonly used as a sound of expression. It may be viewed as inappropriate or impolite.

This illustrates the importance of cultural understanding when interpreting non-verbal sounds. Something as simple as a tongue click can be misunderstood across cultures if you are not aware of the different meanings and norms.

Diaspora and Non-verbal Sounds

Expanding upon the nuanced nature of non-verbal communication, it is essential to consider the impact of diaspora on the evolution and interpretation of these sound signals. As populations migrate and disperse, traditional non-verbal vocalisations are carried to new environments. Within these diasporic communities, these sounds may undergo transformation, blending with or adapting to the auditory landscapes of their host cultures. This process can lead to the creation of hybrid sound signals, reflecting the complex interplay between cultural preservation and adaptation. Conversely, some traditional sounds may be lost or altered due to the pressures of assimilation or the disruption of intergenerational transmission.

A Case of Comparative Cultural Study of Non-verbal Emotions Among Indian and Spanish People

While basic human emotions such as happiness, sadness, anger, fear, and surprise are generally recognised across cultures, the expression and interpretation of these emotions can vary from one culture to another. In an empirical research, Maria Gendron et al. (2014) and her colleagues examine whether or not certain emotions, such as anger, fear, and sadness are recognised across cultures in non-verbal cues. They found accuracy in Himba participants in their test occurred only when foils differed from targets in valence, indicating that the voice can reliably convey affective meaning across cultures, but that perceptions of emotion from the voice are culturally variable.

Table 4.1 Non-verbal emotions among Indian and Spanish people

Emotion	*Indian culture*	*Spanish culture*
Laughing:	Indians commonly laugh louder compared to Middle Eastern people. They laugh loudly and clearly, with wide open mouths. Sometimes they cover their mouth with their hands to make it more polite. Males laugh louder than females. The loud laugh is not traditionally considered polite behaviour for women. When they feel angry and upset, they may just have a cold smile. When trying to control laughter in situations where it's not appropriate, they often bite their tongue or grab it with their teeth and shake their head left and right a bit to hold back their laughter.	Spanish people typically laugh very loudly in friendly environments. It is usually represented as "ja ja ja" or "jajaja." This is similar to "ha ha ha" in English-speaking cultures. In situations where it is not polite to laugh, they usually hide their excitement and emotions. If someone gets annoyed or angry he or she might express laughing like "he-he" or a single laugh like "he-bro." When they feel enjoyment, they laugh like "ja ja ja" or slap each other or push and say "idiote" (means idiot) or "La ver dad" (means really). In funny situations, they chuckle, and it doesn't last very long. In some situations, Spanish people may laugh when they are unhappy or can do nothing with a problem.
Sadness:	Indians, particularly females, may openly cry or weep when they are feeling sad or emotionally overwhelmed. They may have vocalised expressions such as sighing, moaning, or groaning and describing and narrating their emotions and experiences. Indians may use non-verbal and facial expressions that indicate sadness, such as a downcast or pensive look, furrowed brows, teary eyes, or a frown. They may also express sadness through silence and body language such as slouching, crossing their arms, or hunching their shoulders.	Most often expressing sadness for the Spanish is just staying quiet and looking down. In Spanish culture, like most other cultures, it is very common for females to openly cry or weep when they are feeling sad. At the time of sadness, expressions like the following may be said: • "Mi mente": My mind • "No quiero": I don't want to. • "Quiero morir": I want to die. • "Que trijste": How sad.

(*Continued*)

Table 4.1 (Continued)

Emotion	*Indian culture*	*Spanish culture*
Anger:	The expression of anger in India can vary depending on individual personality, upbringing, and social context. They may loudly scream in anger and seldom laugh. Non-verbal expressions of anger can include gestures, facial expressions, and body language. These may include clenched fists, a stern or aggressive facial expression, or an intense gaze. Some individuals may have emotional outbursts when angry, which can involve crying, yelling, or even physical expressions like slamming doors or throwing objects. In many cases, when anger arises within interpersonal relationships, Indians may seek mediation or resolution through communication.	The expression of anger in Spanish culture like several other cultures can vary depending on individual personality and social context. Here are some commonly observed non-verbal cues: raised voice; making forceful hand gestures; facial expressions such as furrowing their brows, squinting their eyes, tightening their lips, or even gritting their teeth; body language such as pacing back and forth, crossing arms, stomping feet; intense eye contact; and quick movements or fidgeting.
Crying:	In Indian culture, the expression of grief and mourning can vary depending on various factors, including regional customs, religious beliefs, and personal preferences. While some individuals may choose to openly express their emotions and cry during mourning periods, others may prefer to control their crying or display their grief in more subdued ways. During ceremonial family gatherings, it is common for people to express their emotions openly, which may include crying, wailing, or lamenting. However, there are also cultural norms that encourage individuals to maintain composure and control their emotions, particularly in public or formal settings.	Spanish people are considered to be romantic. It is not common for males to cry but for females it is normal. They cry in scary or uncomfortable situations and pass away. They tend to cry openly and loudly if somebody passes away. During sadness and crying they may have expressions like these: • “No quiero”: I don’t want to. • “Quiero morir”: I want to die Football is very serious for them, and it is usual for fans to cry if their favourite team loses.

(Continued)

Table 4.1 (Continued)

Emotion	*Indian culture*	*Spanish culture*
Boredom:	When Indians feel bored, they may express their boredom through a combination of verbal and non-verbal cues. For example, during watching a movie, if it is not interesting, they use phrases like "kya hai ye?" (means: "What is it?"). Audible sighs or yawns can be indications of boredom and fatigue. Indians may exhibit signs of restlessness, such as fidgeting, constantly shifting position, or tapping fingers or feet. Avoiding eye contact or having a distant gaze can be a non-verbal sign of boredom. In social gatherings, people cannot easily express their boredom because they have to be polite.	When Spanish people are bored, they may use various non-verbal cues or actions to express their boredom. Some expressions to show boredom include yawning, eye-rolling, sighing, fidgeting, glancing around, checking the time, frequently looking at a watch or smartphone, and avoiding eye contact. They also may say the following phrases: • "Vamos": let's go • "Por fa vor": oh, please. • "Estoy aburrido": I'm bored.
Surprising:	Indians may put their hands on their mouth and say "Uh" and "Arre Wah!" which has no particular meaning, but is often used to indicate intense feelings. They may widen their eyes momentarily, raise their eyebrows to visually convey their astonishment, open their mouth slightly or gasp, place a hand on their chest, cover the mouth, or raise their hands to the head as a reaction to the unexpected.	At the time surprise their eyes open wide and they put their hands on their face and say "La verdad." Some common expressions at the time of surprise include • "La verdad" ("really") • "Ostras" ("Oysters") • "¿A sí?" ("oh, really?" or "Is that so?") • "Guau" ("wow") • "¿Para mí?" ("for me?") • "¿En serio?" ("seriously?"). • - "¿Es una broma?" ("Is it a joke?")
Coughing:	When it comes to coughing, it is mostly symbolic and is often used when someone has revealed a secret. It is a sign like excuse me: for example, in a narrow street and they are walking and someone has blocked their way, so they will cough, as a signal or warning.	Although a sign of illness, it is sometimes used as a non-verbal expression and can have various meanings depending on the context including drawing attention to themselves or expressing their disagreement or disapproval with a situation; showing respect or politeness; and as a conversational filler, similar to using English fillers such as "um" or "uh."

(*Continued*)

Table 4.1 (Continued)

Emotion	*Indian culture*	*Spanish culture*
Yawning:	In India, "bhuts" (spirits) are believed to prefer entering the body through the mouth. Yawning is therefore dangerous because it entails two kinds of risks: either bhuts penetrate the body through the throat, or a part of the soul might escape. Since it would be very difficult to recapture, the recommended practice is to put a hand in front of one's mouth and say "Narayan!" (Good God!), or snap one's fingers to scare the bad spirit away (Loisy, 1921). It is seen as impolite to yawn openly in public, especially during conversations, meetings, or religious ceremonies.	It may be perceived as impolite to yawn in certain social situations, especially in front of people or friends that you do not know. In a social gathering, when a person yawns, others think that they have to leave or stop talking, even if one yawns unintentionally.
Shyness:	Indians indicate shyness with a smile and by looking here and there. In this situation, they talk softer than in normal situations. Also, they hide their smile and sometimes they do not make any sounds.	Several expressions can indicate shyness, including smiling without saying a word; blushing by cheeks turning red; avoiding eye contact; nervous gestures, such as fidgeting, playing with one's hair, or tapping fingers; speaking softly; certain postures such as crossing arms, slouching, or hunching their shoulders. Sometimes they hide their face and mouths and say "no no no no."
Fear and horror:	Fear and horror can be expressed through various non-verbal cues, gestures, and body language including facial expressions (e.g., eyes getting bigger), body language (hold and deep breathing), vocal cues (gasping, screaming, or crying out, and trembling voice), hand gestures (clenching fists, covering the mouth with hands), posture (adopt a defensive posture, such as bringing their knees to their chest). When scared, Indians may invoke their god's name and react with: "Ram Ram Ram." They also make these sounds: "Oh, oie, oyee," and call god's name and it depends on people:" jeash ram, ram, hey bhagwan, hey ma (mother).	Spanish people express fear or horror very much similar to people of other cultures. Nonetheless, certain aspects of their culture can influence their reactions. In Spain, people may use phrases such as "¡Dios mío!" (My God!); "¡Madre mía!" (My mother!); "¡Qué miedo!" (How scary!); or "La ver dad" and "No." They might also cover their mouths with their hands or gasp in surprise. Some individuals may cross themselves as a reflex, particularly those who are more religiously inclined.

(*Continued*)

Table 4.1 (Continued)

Emotion	*Indian culture*	*Spanish culture*
Excitement:	Indians express their excitement by talking and laughing loudly or saying some words like • "Shabash" (well done; bravo). • "Arre wah": it does not have an exact meaning. • "Oh bete": "Oh son". • They also use "maar maar" in a fight which means "hit hit." • arey ye kya hua or areyyyyyyy means: what happened (the length of "areyyyyyyy" usually indicates the intensity of the emotion being expressed).	When something is good and they like it and they get excited, they say "esto" which means "this." Other ways of showing excitement by Spanish people are somehow universal, including clapping hands, jumping up and down, high-five, hugging or embracing, raising fists, and shouting or cheering.
Sighing:	Sighing conveys a range of emotions, including frustration or disappointment, fatigue or exhaustion, resignation, and emotional release.	While sighing is a universal expression that can be used to convey various emotions, including surprise, sadness, or happiness, it is not necessarily specific to Spanish people.
Whistling:	Nodding one's head sideways is generally considered a negative gesture in many parts of India. Even if it is just done to the beat of a song, it is a sign of apathy. The reason for this is that in India, there are more ruffians and rascals among the beggars and loafers who whistle the most, especially those who want to attract a lady's attention or say something to her. That's why it has acquired a negative connotation. But it is also used to express happiness or enjoyment.	Whistling is not a polite act in common. As a nonverbal expression, however, it can have various meanings and interpretations, including attention-seeking, appreciation, and surprise, expressing surprise, and catcalling, which is considered inappropriate in public.

Here in this section, a comparative cultural study of non-verbal emotions among Indian and Spanish people is briefly examined as a case study to show how individuals from these two cultures express and interpret emotions through non-verbal cues. The data was collected from a series of free interviews with individuals from the two cultures. This comparison aids in finding a set of similarities and contrasts in emotional expressions between the two.

Non-verbal cues help contextualise and interpret verbal messages within a cultural framework. The advent of technologies such as television, the internet, social media, and smartphones has drastically increased the exposure of people to different cultures and traditions from around the world. This constant exchange of information has significantly changed the degree of interpreting non-verbal emotions in the cross-cultural domain. In the past, people relied mainly on face-to-face interactions or written correspondence to communicate with individuals from other cultures. This limited exposure made it difficult for individuals to accurately interpret the non-verbal cues and gestures of others. However, with the rise of global communication platforms, people now have access to a wealth of information and can observe how individuals from other cultures express their emotions through gestures, body language, and facial expressions. Yet, many people would rather emphasise things that give them a sense of their cultural identity, such as clothing, way of eating and drinking, decorating their home and listening to their ethnic music. This preference for cultural identity can be seen as a way for individuals to connect with their roots, heritage, and history. It can also be a way for people to express themselves and show pride in their background.

Note

1 Matter of the heart

Chapter 5

Music

Introduction

There are numerous definitions for music each of which tries to signify the notion of music, and yet it is open to new definitions by today and future scholars. Music is organised sound in a given time, but the way it is organised and appreciated defines many things, including the tastes and values of the people who create and perceive it. Such tastes and values designate a distinguished identity to music. In creating and playing music, people consider both situational uses and underlying functions of music. "Use refers to the situation in which music is employed in human action; function concerns the reasons for its employment and particularly the broader purpose which it serves" (Merriam, 1964, p. 210). Both use and function play a great role in shaping the musical culture of every society.

Video game music has evolved significantly over the past four decades, transcending its initial novelty to become a vital component of contemporary culture and scholarship. In their examination of the evolution of game sound, Melanie Fritsch and Tim Summers (2021, p. 1) begin with a vivid depiction of the history of game music:

> Pong game by Atari initially released in 1972: Three "bips" disrupted the silence – this is how a written history of game sound might start. These famous "bips" in three different pitches occurred when players hit the white pixel representing the ball with the controllable white bar representing the bat, when the ball bumped from the upper or lower border or when the ball went off screen in the first widely commercially successful arcade game.

From the simple melodic loops of early games like Space Invaders to the intricate orchestral scores of modern titles, video game music now encompasses a vast array of styles and instrumentation, engaging millions of listeners worldwide.

> Pong game by Atari initially released in 2021: No longer a novelty within electronic music technology, nor a poor relation of film music, game music

DOI: 10.4324/9781003591399-6

engages huge audiences and large budgets and is the site of innovative scholarship. As well as being a crucial component of the audiovisual interactive experience of video gaming, game music has also had a marked impact on broader popular culture.

In this chapter, we depart from a traditional music analysis approach to some extent to explore how musical sounds serve as designed elements within game environments, rather than solely expressions of personal artistry. We will examine the practical application of understanding cultural sound signals, acknowledging the potential for both authentic representation and cultural misinterpretation in the digital age. Recognising that game development teams often collaborate with external composers, this chapter aims to bridge the gap between theoretical analysis and practical application, providing insights into ethical sound design practices and the responsible use of cultural audio elements, particularly in light of the evolving landscape of cultural knowledge in the 21st century.

The study of music in culture does not follow the same path as the study of the sciences. In the process of solving a problem in science, there are two components: "scientist" and a phenomenon outside him called "problem." In contrast, in music study, we face an interactive activity in which three components play a role: "musicologist," "dynamic phenomenon of music," and "creator of music."

Now, the most crucial question will be "How can we be sure that our perception of a piece of music is similar to the way people of that culture may perceive it?" Do not expect a definite answer to this question; maybe never but this does not eliminate or weaken our aim. We look for clues to understand the mystery of humans, and we can find nothing helpful like music. In this difficult task, however, we have a gift to stay hopeful; we are human ourselves, and this is a great chance. We experience passion, ecstasy, seduction, fear, desire for immortality, and above all "love," which is the main secret of music-making.

If all the constituent elements of music are in accordance with the cultural assets of a listener he or she will feel it is from their culture. However, the sense that a piece of music belongs to one's own culture is not absolute; this means that when one listens to two pieces, he or she may feel that one of them is relatively *closer* to them than the other one. The elements which make music sound familiar to one's cultural or social identity are a combination of musicological structure and cultural characteristics of that piece. The model presented in this study is based on those two aspects.

Musicological Structure

Various musical elements build the formal structure of every piece of music. We can make a list of musical elements that take part in the formation of music, but the significance of every element in shaping music differs from one culture to another. For instance, the "tonal framework" of *maqāmāt* and "prosodic meters" employed by traditional singers are considered to be central in the configuration of central Asian music while "complex rhythmic patterns" and "polymetric" are in the heart of percussive music of Central Africa. Here are ten main musical elements which contribute to shaping musical structure in general:

- Pitch, interval, tonal and modal framework
- Melodic shape and movements
- Rhythmic and metric structure
- Dynamic and expressions
- Phrasal structure
- Timbre and instrumentations
- Harmonic structure
- Texture and vertical relations
- Overall formal structure
- Lyrical structure

Pitch, Interval, Tonal, and Modal Framework

Pitch is the human perception of the *relative* highness or lowness of a particular sound. Music comes to exist by a set of pitches which are distinguished from each other by frequency differentiations. However, the role of intonation and pitch deviations of the performers are much more important than the mathematical ratios of the pitches within any scale system. For instance, deep vibrations and bending are vital characteristics of Indian music performance. One can hardly find a plain pitch in a performance of Indian classical music, since every single pitch is played by distinguishable articulations and vibrations. This fact is clearly seen in the structure of Indian traditional musical instruments like dilruba, esraj, veena, and sitar in which frets are curved and sit far from the fingerboard to facilitate the performer with deep vibrations and bending.

Some artists have adapted Western instruments to capture the essence of Indian music. For instance, Shintai, a Belgian musician, modified his guitar to resemble the Indian veena by replacing the frets on the fingerboard.

The rows of pitches with distinctive intervals among them are used as the tonal or modal framework of music. The *tuning system* is an important factor in most musical cultures. Even tuning in live music on the stage of Western countries is constantly adjusted by inhabited ears. The strategy of applying pitches and other musical elements to configure music developed over the musical life of every culture and eventually have made a musical system to be considered as a musical heritage of that culture, including *ragā* in India, *dastgāh* in Iran and Azerbaijan, *shash maqām* in Uzbek and Tajik music, and *maqām* in the Arab world.

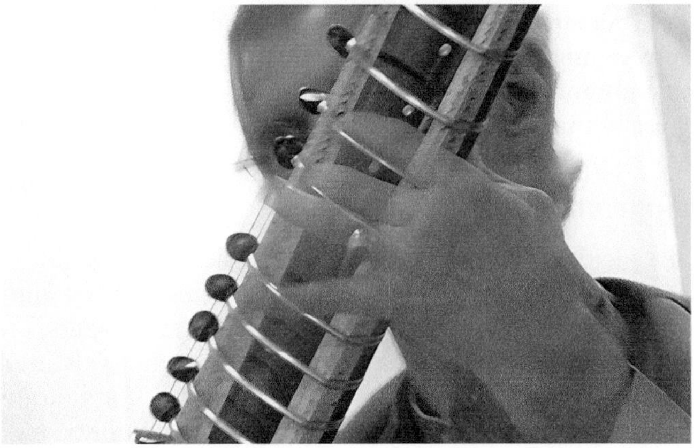

Figure 5.1 Frets in a sitar are curved and sit high enough above the neck to allow for deep vibrations and bending (photo by the author)

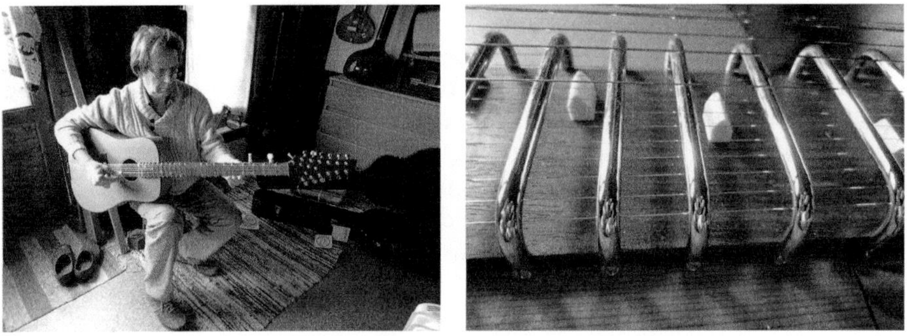

Figure 5.2 Veena-Guitar developed by Shintai to play Indian music on guitar (photo: www.sitarfactory.be)

Each pitch within a scale serves a particular function. To set functions of every degree in a scale in tonal music, we need first to stabilise tonality. It is essential to know how to highlight the tonic or root note, as well as the dominant, while also creating a sense of tension and release in a manner that reflects the practices of musicians within that cultural context. Emphasising the tonic can be achieved through various techniques, particularly through repetition and by positioning the tonic as the ultimate destination for melodic movement. When melodies seem aimless, it means the functions of degrees have not been established. In Western tonal music, the emphasis on tonal degrees mostly benefits from harmonic arrangements while in Indian, Iranian, Turkish, and Arab music it comes to exist through the melody line and the drone[1] (particularly in Indian music). In simple words, the cultural identity of music very much depends on the way music makers establish the tonal or modal settings and the strategy they undertake to constitute the functions of every degree within a scale or mode in the process of music creation.

Melodic Shape and Movements

Melody is the incident and arrangement of musical sounds along the line of time that is perceived to be unified based on cultural norms and aesthetics. The structure of every melody is configured by several elements, including the range of tones; register of tones; the complexity of intervals used; contour; phrasing; motific or non-motific structure; rhythmic configuration; repetition transformation and development of materials, and so on. The tradition of crafting melodies using the aforementioned elements, along with the strategies employed by musicians to incorporate them, plays a crucial role in shaping cultural musical identity. In the previous section, we explored the significance of pitches and intervals in the musical traditions of various cultures. In the following sections, we will examine the rhythmic structure, phrasing, and theme developments. Here we focus on melodic movements and contour as one of the central elements of melody.

Melodic contour or melodic map is defined as the sequence of ups and downs in the pitches of the melody. Contour is known to be a highly attention-catching aspect of melodies, an aspect that even infants perceive, and plays a significant role in recognising melody (Trehub et al., 1984). Melodic contour is among the characteristic features of melody, which is largely seen in music analysis literature wherever the melody is taken into account for analysis (e.g., Densmore, 1918; Herzog, 1928; McAllester, 1949; Merriam, 1967; Roberts, 1933; Adams, 1976). Herzog (1950, p. 1047) in a review of song classification techniques writes:

> the most suggestive method which is occasionally proposed, is that by melodic contour. This method seems very worth testing on a large scale since often the melodic contour turns out to be the most stable element in melodies which have been in the process of differentiation.

A rather big chunk of Charles R. Adams study "Melodic Contour Typology" also addresses this issue. He sees melodic contour, which comprises several features, as a very central issue in music analysis:

> The differential concern with melodic contour raises questions concerning its role in melodic analysis, its significance in musical description, its cross-cultural applicability, and comparative utility. It can be assumed that a well-defined concept of melodic contour would provide a useful analytical tool and a valid baseline for comparative research.
>
> (1976, p. 180)

Adams (1976, p. 195) defines melodic contour as the product of distinctive relationships among the minimal boundaries of a melodic segment. Melodic segment refers to any series of differentiated pitches (motives, phrases, songs, sections between junctures in intoned speech, and so on). *Minimal boundaries* are those pitches that are considered necessary and sufficient to delineate a melodic segment, with respect to its temporal aspect (beginning-end) and its tonal aspect (tonal range). Bounding a series of pitches by an *initial pitch*, a *final pitch*, a *highest pitch*, and a *lowest pitch*, satisfies these conditions, while defining fewer or more boundaries does not.

Introducing the melodic formation of all inhabited cultures of the world in a single volume is neither practically possible nor meets the aim of this book. Here I report the structure of melodic contour in Iranian classical music, the field of my expertise, as a case to show how such examination can shed light on characteristics of musical culture.[2]

Typically studies on Iranian music, particularly issues related to its melodic aspects, are very much occupied by the discussion of modal systems of *dastgāh-ha*[3] and the arrangements and functions of notes and their alteration within a tetrachord and pentachord. The cultural listener of Iranian music, however, pays little or no attention to microtones and their complicated arrangements in a mathematical way. In fact, what grasps his or her main attention is the melodic arrangements of the piece coming into existence through melodic movement and rhythmic activities.

In a comprehensive five-year study of the melodic structure of Iranian music, I developed a new analytical tool tailored to the unique characteristics of Iranian classical music. The new tool led to new approaches to analysing melodic configurations. I utilised it to examine the melodic contours of 106 *gūsheh-ha*[4] within the *dastgāhi* system of Iranian music. This approach can be adapted for similar studies, particularly in musical traditions that employ analogous systems, such as Turkish *mokāms*, Arabic *maqāms*, and Indian *rāgā*.

While there are numerous musical features to explore in the study of melody, I will primarily focus on three fundamental elements that shape *gūsheh-ha*: directions, intervals, and time values. The emotional response elicited in listeners from each melody arises from the interplay of these three elements, as well as the performers' interpretation of them. The functioning of these features within a musical piece can be illustrated through various approaches, each offering its own set of advantages and disadvantages, which I will briefly outline here.

One of the common approaches to describing the outline of melody in a piece is verbal narration. In the verbal narration method, the story of melodic events is verbally narrated. Charlotte Johnson (1964) uses this method to describe the Navaho corn-grinding songs. Here I present an example of describing the melodic events in *gūsheh darāmad* in *dastgāh shūr*.[5]

The melody starts from the sub-tonic and wonders between the tonic and the supertonic. After some moments of wondering melody settles on the tonic

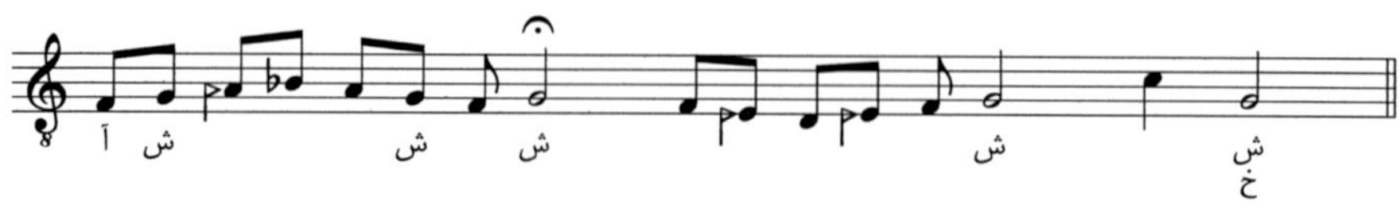

Figure 5.3 Sample of melodic movement in *darāmad shūr* (Pourtorāb et al., 2012, pp. 39–66)

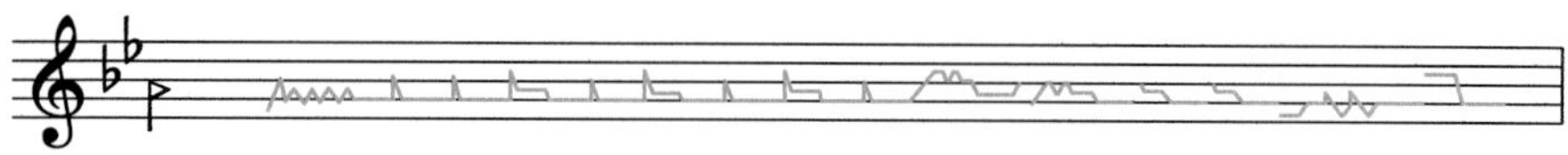

Figure 5.4 Using graphic lines to demonstrate the melodic contour of *darāmad shūr*

and takes a rest there. The whole things repeat this time in a higher degree with minor variations in ornamentation, but it does not give a proper feeling of the settlement at the end of the phrase as this time it finishes on the second rather than the first degree (this degree plays the role of real sensible in descending scale of shūr). In the end, the melody repeats one note lower and gives the listener a good feeling of finishing.

The problem with the verbal narration method is that it is lengthy. The style is somehow poetic and therefore might be considered a bit inaccurate.

One of the less popular ways of showing the melodic outlook is presenting a summary of elementary notes of the melody on a staff notation in an abstract way. This approach was used by Pourtorāb and his colleagues (2012, pp. 39–66). Here is an example.[6]

The above approach of indicating the main melodic outline of *gūsheh-ha* comprises some advantages and disadvantages. This approach is capable of representing the melodic configuration in a very precise manner concerning intervals, time values, and other musical aspects. Nonetheless, this approach is incapable of demonstrating the listener's perception of emotion and overall perception of melodies which sometimes are very far from any notation outlook.

Another limitation of this method lies in its reliance on tools that closely resemble those of conventional notation systems, which are typically employed for detailed descriptions of entire pieces. Once we consider the purpose of the authors used this system to illustrate the essence of melodies in *gūsheh-ha* – so-called melody types – another problem is revealed. The various versions of *gūsheh-ha* in Iran, passed down through generations via an oral tradition, are known as *revāyat*. Each *revāyat*, as reported by master musicians, includes their own interpretations and inspirations. This system of using conventional notation to represent the melodic contour of each *gūsheh* may not recognise the structural elements from momentary additive features included based on the taste of the master performers in their reports, as it focuses too much on precise details rather than the abstract nature of the melodic contour of *gūsheh-ha*.

One of the most common methods employed by musicologists to demonstrate melodic contour is the use of graphic lines. In the figure below, I present the melodic contour of the *darāmad shūr*.

As shown in the figure above, this method of illustrating melodic contours offers the advantage of enabling simultaneous observation of both the direction of melodic movement and the associated time values. The melodic direction in *darāmad shūr* and other *gūsheh-ha* in this *dastgāh* follows a level or occasionally wavelike path around a central tone referred to as the *shāhed* (sweetheart). The key tones in *shūr* classify it as a *dastgāh* characterised by descending scales, where the second degree (in this case, A *Koron*)[7] acts as the primary sensible or leading note. As a result, the melody often transitions from A *Koron* to G in its melodic structure.

The method of using graphic lines for representing melodic movements is still an adequate way of analysing melodies. However, sometimes musicologists need to analyse melodic movements in a series of tunes or pieces for the purpose of comparison and generalisation of melodic structure in various works of a composer, a musical system, or a musical culture. In such cases, the graphic methods have some limitations, particularly if the number of pieces to be analysed rises. I created a system to analyse and categorise the melodic movements in a large number of Iranian tunes, allowing for a systematic study of the melodic structures in traditional music.

Initially, I organised and structured different potential patterns a melody could follow in its linear progression. The table below displays the organisation of various melodic motions. This classification draws on concepts from Duncan M. Courvoisier's work in 1957.

In the following step, I analysed the key *gushes-ha* of Iranian music (main traditional repertory) and classified the melodic form of each into one of the

Table 5.1 Classification of various melodic movements (Azadehfar after Courvoisier, 1957)

Melodic movements									
Pendulum	Arc		Level (with very limited tonal material)	Descending			Ascending		
	Inverted Arc	Proper Arc		Straight	Sequential	Terrace	Straight	Sequential	Terrace

Table 5.2 Melodic movements of the main *gūsheh-ha* in *dastgāh shūr*

Main Gūsheh-ha		Melodic movements									
			Arc			Descending			Ascending		
Name of dastgāh or āvāz	*Name of gūsheh*	*Pendulum*	*Inverted Arc*	*Proper Arc*	*Level (with limited movements)*	*Straight*	*Sequential*	*Terrace*	*Straight*	*Sequential*	*Terrace*
Dastgāh Shūr	darāmad	○			○	●					
	Rohāb	○			●						○
	Zirkeh-salmak						●				
	Salmak						●				
	Mollānāzī	●					○	○			
	Uzzāl	●									
	Safā				●						
	Dobeytī						●				
	Bozorg			●	○						
	Kuchak				●						
	Khārā				●						
	Razavī	○			●						
	Shahnāz	●							○		

sense of their musical culture. However, a systematic study is needed to categorise musical elements and conduct a comparative analysis. My proposed approach aids in examining the qualitative phenomenon of melodic movements to better understand the formal musical structure of this tradition.

The following chart summarises the outcome of my examination of melodic movements of *gūsheh-ha* of Iranian music – only a portion of that is presented here for space saving. The chart highlights the overall characteristics of melodic movements in 106 *gūsheh-ha* from seven *dastgāh-ha* and their five auxiliary *āvāz-ha* in Iranian classical music.

The salient classification of melodic movements in the formation of melodies of Iranian classical music can be seen in the above chart.

The use of sustained melodic contour as the primary melodic structure and sequential descending movements as secondary elements can evoke certain emotional responses from listeners of this music. Since ascending melodic

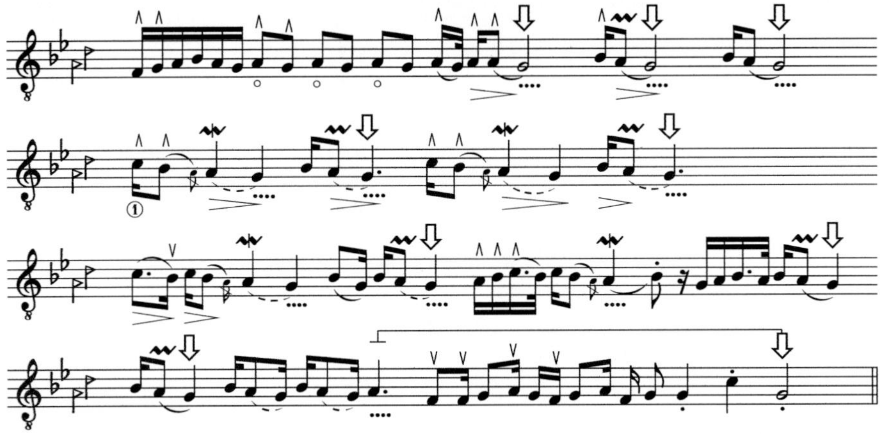

Figure 5.5 Darāmad aval in *dastgāh shūr* (During, 2010, p. 15)

ten types of movements outlined in the table above. I identified two distinct categories of melodic movements for each *gūsheh*: structural and momentary. Structural movements are marked with the symbol ●, while momentary movements are denoted by ○ in the classification table. Drawing on my expertise as a musician with a background in Iranian tradition, I distinguished between the structural elements and momentary musical occurrences by comparing various versions of collections by different Iranian masters.

In this project, the melodic contour of Iranian classical music was exemplified by analysing a total of 106 *gūsheh-ha*. Due to constraints, not all 106 *gūsheh-ha* and their tables can be presented here. Instead, one out of the 12 tables will be showcased, focusing on the *gūsheh-ha* of the *dastgāh shūr*. Prior to that, a gūsheh in Western notation will be provided as an illustrative example.

The table below outlines the melodic movements of the mentioned example and the other *gūsheh-ha* in *dastgāh shūr* as presented in my proposed method for representing melodic movements.

Upon closer examination of the melodic patterns in *dastgāh shūr*, it is evident that the majority of melodies tend to follow a level trajectory within a narrow tonal range. Unlike other *dastgāh-ha*, *shūr* does not typically feature leaps or ascending movements in its melodic formations. Instead, pendulum motions and sequential descending melodies are commonly utilised. While arch shape movements are prevalent in other *dastgāh-ha*, they are rare in *shūr*. Overall, there are fewer translational movements and more rolling movements in the melodic structure of gūsheh-ha in dastgāh *shūr*.

There is no better approach than attending events within the society for listening, learning, performing music, and experiencing everyday life to make

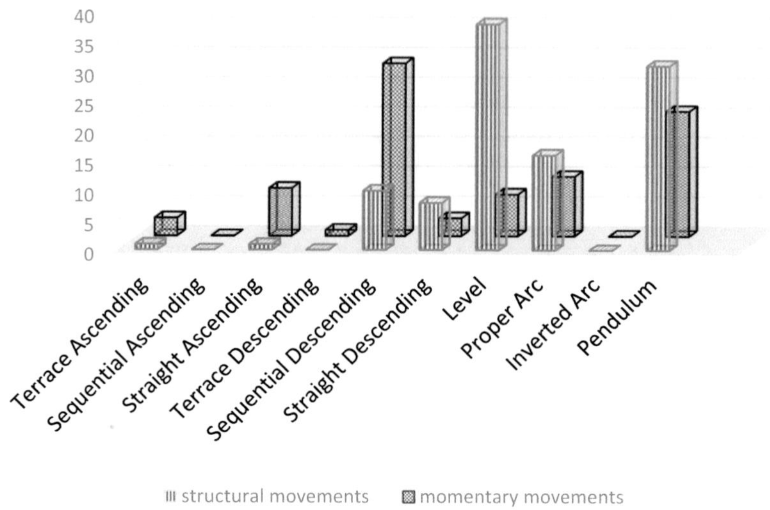

Figure 5.6 The summary of examining melodic movements in 106 *gūsheh-ha* of Iranian music

movements are not popular in the melodic structure of *dastgāh-ha*, people with the habit of listening to joyful ascending melodies in their own cultures, describe Iranian classical music as being somehow "sad music." As ascending melodic movements are not commonly found in the melodic patterns of *dastgāh-ha*, individuals accustomed to ascending melodies in their own cultural music may describe Iranian classical music as being somehow "sad or melancholic music." However, for Iranian listeners, the concept of "*ḥuzn*" represents a unique type of sadness stemming from the anguish of separation from an eternal love, dating back to the expulsion of Adam and Eve from paradise. This type of melancholy music is appreciated and passed down through generations in Iranian culture.

Presenting the technical specifications accompanied by the cultural characteristics in the above case showed how combining music analysis along with cultural studies helps in drawing musical identity beneficial to music composers in creating melodies for any given scene – whether drama or games – in accordance with cultural norms and aesthetics.[8]

Rhythmic and Metric Structure

Rhythm is the "organization of time in parts accessible to the senses" (Heusler, 1925, p. 17 cited in Sachs, 1953, p. 15). Parts consist of durations or time spans which form a cohesive cluster called a *rhythmic group*. But the individual who organises parts of sounds along the line of time makes the outcome unique to him/her – and in an upper layer his/her culture. The basic musical shape of a piece is established through the process of configuring rhythmic groups to project a sense that some notes go with other notes, and that these groups themselves form larger units. Two other crucial concepts in studying rhythm are *metre* and *tempo*. Metre refers to the listener's sense of pulsation inferred from regularity in accruing musical events to which he/she can steadily tap or clap. Tempo is the sense of speed in recurring metric accents or beats and is generally measured as the number of beats per minute. Justin London (2001, p. 283) says "when a piece begins, its metre and tempo are usually not known to the listener, and so the listener must make metric inferences from the pattern of durations and stresses that are given." London believes this stage usually takes place quickly and without difficulty. "Once the metre is established it takes on a life of its own; the listener may then project a sense of accent onto an event even if it is not otherwise marked by duration, dynamics, contour, or harmonic change." It seems London is describing an inhabited Western listener listening to Western music in this statement. Conversely, if we think of a complex metric cycle in Javanese Gamelan music, it will be far from ease of comprehending for an outsider audience. In Gamelan music, the cyclic structure of meter is iterated and punctuated by the sounds of various sized gongs, and the main metrical accent is placed at the *end* of metrical cycles instead of the beginning, as would typically happen in Western music.

Another distinctive feature of metric configuration in the music of various cultures is consistent metric pulsation versus metric irregularity. While Western pop and classical music mostly benefit from fixed metric structures, a large chunk of music in West and Central Asia is performed in free or stretchable metre. The term "free metre," in general, suggests a structure variable in accordance with the performer's wishes. The listener's perception process in free-metered pieces is different from the way fixed-meter pieces are perceived. In fixed-meter pieces, the meter acts like a reference grid over which rhythmic materials are understood. When there is no fixed meter, rhythmic materials and musical phrases should be perceived by the listener on their own instead of being perceived in the metric context. In the absence of metric regularity and its relevant pulsation, some other musical elements provide the consistency of the material to aid the listener with the comprehension of musical events. For instance, regularity in phrasing can provide a kind of coherence throughout the piece. The regularity of phrasing is usually delivered by the symmetry of proportions and the use of imitation through question and response in the configuration of musical sentences. On such occasions, every phrase is balanced by its immediately following phrase. The second phrase is not necessarily an exact imitation of the first phrase in length and pattern. As the first phrase becomes longer, the responding phrase has more tolerance for diminishing or extending.

Some cultures benefit from a great treasure of rhythmic patterns and metric cycles used as raw materials for music creation. *Tāla* In Indian music, *iqā'* in Arabic and Persian music, and *usūl* in Turkish music, for instance, are a treasury of rhythmic cycles used in the formation of both pre-composed and improvised music. In the traditional system of education of learning music, a student first memorises the rhythmic cycles kinetically by striking the knees with the hands. Each culture in the above list has its standard pronounceable vocables built from combinations of the syllables to orally demonstrate every cyclic pattern. There are also some shared rhythmic patterns in the music culture of Central and West Asia, North Africa, India, and even East Europe. In a project, I investigated similarities and differences between *tāla* and *iqā'* to find a sharing ground between Indian rhythmic cycles and Persian musical timing. I analysed nine cycles in the primary project from which I will provide one example here to demonstrate my above statements. Next, I will provide definitions of pulse levels in cycles from both musical cultures.

Pulse levels in cycles of īqā'	*Pulse levels in tālā*	*Equal term in English*
dowr	avart	cycle
afā'īl	-	phrase
	vibhāg	motif
naqareh	*mātrā*	beat

We are comparing *Tīntāl*, the most commonly used *tālā* in north Indian classical music, with *Khafīf thaqīl* from the collection of *īqā'* cycles in Persian and Arabic music. The name *Tīntāl* signifies the three claps in its *vibhāgs* structure, which is symmetrical and composed of four *vibhāgs* of four *mātrās* each – represented by a clap, clap, wave, and clap. The following table illustrates the comparison between the structure of *Tīntāl* and the *īqā'* of *Khafīf thaqīl.*

Table 5.3 Comparison of *Tintāl* cycle in Indian music and *Khafīf thaqīl* in Persian music

Tīntāl	1 2 3 4	5 6 7 8	9 10 11 12	13 14 15 16
	> Clap	> Clap		> Clap
	X	2	0	3
	dhā dhin dhin dhā	dhā dhin dhin dhā	dhā tin tin tā	tā dhin dhin dhā
Khafīf thaqīl	Tan Tana	Tan Tana	Tan Tana	Tan Tana
	>			>
	- ∪ ∪	- ∪ ∪	- ∪ ∪	- ∪ ∪

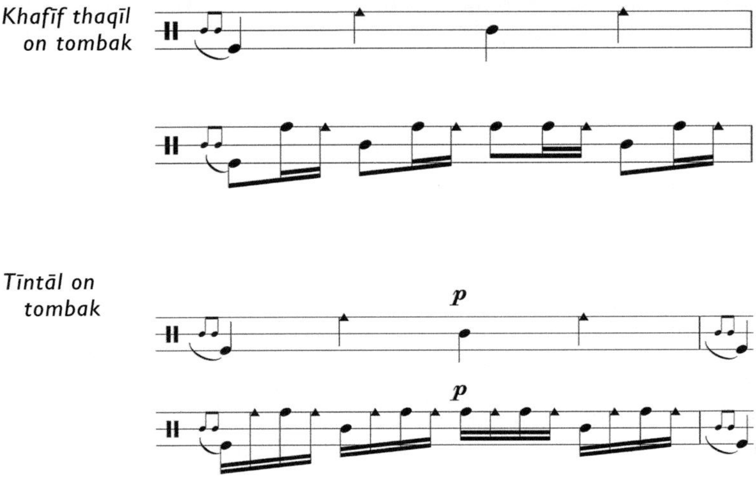

Figure 5.7 Tintāl cycle in Indian music and Khafīf thaqīl in Persian music presented in tombak notation

According to the table above, the structure of both cycles is similar in most aspects, except for the fifth beat, which is accented in *tīntāl* but unaccented in *Khafīf thaqīl*. Below is a proposal for playing both cycles in *tombak* notation.[9]

In summarising the examination of *iqā‘* cycles and *tālā* time cycles, I would categorise the relationship at three levels: 1) *tālās* that perfectly match *īqā‘* cycles; 2) *tālās* that can be adjusted slightly to match cycles of īqā‘; and 3) *tālās* that have no similar time cycle in *īqā‘* system. This comparison can help composers create hybrid music by combining rhythmic patterns from both cultures or emphasise the uniqueness of one culture by using cycles unique to that culture.[10]

Dynamics and Expressions

Dynamic structure plays a decisive role in the identity of performance styles and music schools. Musical dynamics relates to everything concerning loudness and event emphasis in music. When musicians use dynamics to intensify the articulacy of their performance, they have to decide when and why they apply loudness, softness, crescendo, decrescendo, or any other means of emphasis. Dynamics give perspective to what we watch and what we hear. Sounds become louder as we move closer to the source of sounds. This fact helps to give a sense of depth to the music. There is a common tendency to link accents to dynamics; however, recent studies make a distinction among various types of accents and consider metric accents as fundamentally a cognitive phenomenon and rhythmic accents, a structural entity that comes to exist independent of any external intensification (see Lerdahl & Jackendoff, 1983).

There is more than intensifying versus softness in the issue of dynamics. One of the leading scholars in the issue of dynamics is Hugo Riemann (1849–1919). He discusses the issue of phrasing based on the notion of music dynamics and agogics.

> Riemann links dynamics to changes affecting a variety of musical parameters, prizmarily rhythm but also melodic contour and harmony. In addition to metrical-rhythmic disposition, melodic contour affects the interpretive use of dynamics. Ascending melodies with *crescendo* imply "increased life-force with diminishing mass (expanding upward)," while ascending melodies with *diminuendo* imply "decreasing life-force (dissipation)"; analogous qualities were assigned to descending melodies that *crescendo* or *diminuendo*. Even rests have dynamic value; they indicate a growth or decline in the life-force established contextually by the melodic contour and phrasing. Interior rests (those within a phrase as opposed to at its beginning or end) sustain the energy of the ongoing musical activity.
>
> (Rothfarb, 2002, pp. 935–6)

Table 5.4 Two different dynamic contours in a sentence in different English dialects

Native English dialect	*Sample sentence*	*Dynamic shape of the sample sentence*
American:	Are you hungry?	
British and Australian:	Are you hungry?	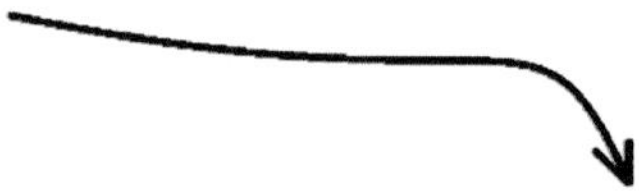

In contrast to other musical elements that are open to unrestricted innovations, there are limitations to using the loudness and softness of accompanied music in films, TV shows, and video games. Watching TV or playing video games usually takes place at home where loud sound bothers others and, indeed, household noises do not let the soft sounds be clearly heard. The limitations are considerably less in cinemas that are exclusively designed for attending to nothing but watching a film. We are bound to a limited range of loudness and softness of the music and virtually every other audio track.

Analysis of dynamic structure captures less attention in music scholarships, and there is a lack of analytical tools for any deep exemption and analysis. In a broad view, the analysis of dynamics and its related features can take place on two different levels: "micro dynamics" and "macro dynamics." At the micro-dynamic level, we study the dynamic structure from a tone envelope – in the phases of attack, decay, sustain, and release – to the dynamic shape of phrasal elements, including figures, motives, phrases, etc. At the macro dynamic level, we look at a broader plot of the dynamic map in the entire piece and its main parts. Micro dynamics instructed by signs and graphics such as *f*, *mf*, *p*, *pp*, and so forth normally appear on a note or a group of notes in the staff notations. However, the macro dynamics are implemented by the sense of conductors and performers and are rarely indicated on notations.

Dynamic is a "relative" phenomenon. It means a single tone played in *pianissimo* in one instrument – trumpet for instance – could relatively be louder than the same tone played in *forte* in another instrument – flute for instance. Performing a crescendo by a musician may be very different from performing the same crescendo by a musician of a different culture. Moreover, dynamics are not normally the same in different parts of polyphonic pieces. Typically, every part that takes the role of delivering the main melody sets louder than accompanied parts. Axel Berndt and Tilo Hähnel (2010) suggest a dynamic model for both micro and macro dynamic maps in an article that is worth reading.

Musical styles of musicians in cultures that give more freedom to the dynamics are very diverse compared to the musical styles of musicians in cultures that have tight restrictions on the dynamic structure of pieces. For an outsider, though, capturing the musical identity of the first group is much harder than apprehending the musical structure of the former group. In some cultures including East Asians' dynamics is an important issue in traditional pedagogical systems. While Westerners most often think Chinese music is loud, the dynamic is an important characteristic of music in various genres and regions of China. For instance, the northern style is more dynamic and energetic than the southern style which is softer and more graceful. Any kind of music that is played outdoors such as music for the *suona* is loud and piercing, and most of the *qin* zither music and lyric songs are naturally soft. Players of *pipa* are capable of expressing a full range of dynamics. A student of *pipa* needs to pay special attention to her music teacher to maintain the correct dynamic structure of every lesson and is frequently corrected by her music instructor to deliver appropriate dynamics and expressions in the course of a performance.

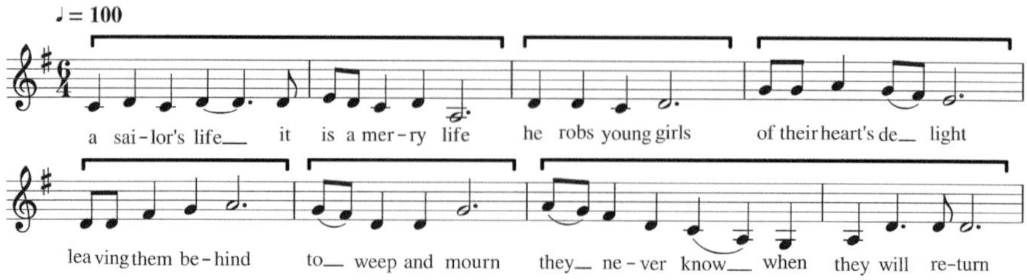

Figure 5.8 The English folk song "A Sailor's Life" is configured based on two kinds of motives: short motives in the length of one bar and long motives in the length of two bars (*after* Watts & Morrissey, 2019, p. 127)

The final issue I discuss here is the power of language and dialect in shaping the dynamic characteristics of music. The grammar of a language, as we will see in the following section, plays an understandable role in the outline of musical phrases, and the sonar structure of language plays a crucial role in the configuration of melodic contour, rhythmic structure, and musical dynamics. The dynamic setting of languages and dialects comes to exist by putting stress on specific syllables while putting no stress on the other syllables and rising and falling the voice pressure over the entire sentence. For this reason, the dynamic shape of languages is examined in two lyres: the syllabic structure of the words and the dynamic shape of the sentences. I can compare words to motives and language sentences to musical sentences. So dynamic structure of a motif can be related to the accentual formation of words and the dynamic form of musical sentences may be affected by the dynamic contour of language sentences. See the following example to see how a very simple sentence presented in different English dialects makes two entirely different dynamic contours.

A deep investigation into the language and dialect of indigenous people of a culture sheds light on the dynamic structure of their music which significantly helps to figure out the musical formation of that culture. The musical identity of every culture is very much affected by the way those elements act in musical creations and appreciations.

Music	*Language*
tone	phoneme
figure	syllable
motif	word
phrase	phrase
sentence	sentence
period	verse
theme section	paragraph
movement	chapter
piece	volume

Phrasal Structure

Phrasing refers to how the sounds *relate* to each other to make groups. The interrelation of sounds to configure a group is a notion that is constituted in the mind of the listener and may not necessarily be visible on staff notations in any direct way. Phrasing is configured in different layers in a hierarchical outline from a motif to the entire piece. Phrasing in music is very much similar to phrasing in language. Syllables form words, words configure phrases and sentences, sentences make paragraphs and paragraphs make chapters, and they go on to make an entire volume. Here is a summary of this similarity:

Please note that the link made between music phrasing and language phrasing in the above table is a free comparison just to give an idea of how phrasing is shaped from the smallest unit to the biggest chunk. Though, the comparison underlines the crucial influence of the language structure on the configuration of music phrasing – no matter lyrical or instrumental music – in every culture.

Grouping follows a set of principles known as Gestalt[11] laws. Gestalt laws describe how the human mind recognises features to group objects, subjects, and whatever is perceivable by our brain. The most important principles are *proximity*, *similarity*, and good *continuation*. The principle of *proximity* refers to a situation in which two or more elements are perceived as a whole when they are perceptually close (e.g., successive tones with no rest or gap among them); the principle of *similarity* is when two or more elements are perceived as a whole because they have similar perceptual features (e.g., same tones and time values in a successive row); and *good continuation* happens when a number of elements are perceived as a whole (e.g., successive tones which shape a musical phrase). Music makers and performers – intendedly or unintendedly – use coherence principles to assist the listeners with a comprehensible and enjoyable music appreciation.

If we accept the basic musical elements (duration, pitch, harmony, instrumentation, etc.) as the material that produces musical stimuli in general, the way of using them is marked by differences of human musical habits within society. A Persian listener, for instance, demands long gaps between musical phrases to consider the philosophical and sophisticated meanings which the musician is meant to deliver – particularly in lyrical music. As a young student learning Persian music, my teacher often emphasised the importance of creating space between musical phrases and developing the skill to know where to pause. I was encouraged to deeply reflect on the meaning of the poems I was singing and playing in order to deliver a coherent musical experience to the audience and maintain the integrity of the overall composition. This idea somewhat brings the suggestion of Cooper and Meyer (1960, p. 1) to mind: "to experience rhythm is to group separate sounds into structured patterns." The intention of the Persian master performer is to guide the listener's attempts to perceive rhythmic groupings. In Persian music, the breaks between rhythmic groups are so pronounced that native musicians often do not feel the need to indicate the ends of each group by rests or greater note values. I presented an example of that along with some other examples of the impact of social habits in rhythmic groupings and metric divisions from India, Bahrain, and Egypt in my earlier book *Rhythmic Structure in Iranian Music* which I will not revisit here for brevity.

"A Sailor's Life" is an English folk song traced back to the 18th century and collected by W. Percy Merrick in 1899 from Henry Hills of Lodsworth in Sussex. The song tells the story of a girl pursuing to find her lover. The lover was a sailor that tragically drowned in the sea. The song is about the girl's mourning the loss of the sailor. At the notation, I indicated the musical phrasing of the song.

As it is seen from the above notation, two kinds of phrases are used in the configuration of this folk song, short motives (one bar long) and long motives (two bars long). Configuring musical pieces based on different lengths of motives leads to a more complex structure compared to constructing pieces based on motives with the same lengths. We can see similar outcomes when phrases are shaped by the interconnection of single or multiple motives, too. Every phrase is shaped by joining two or more motives. In a broad view, I categorise musical phrases into single-core, dual-core, and multiple-core phrases. When only one motif and its repetition constructs the phrase, it will be a single-core phrase; when two different motives join together to make a musical phrase. it will be a dual-core phrase, and when more than two different motives are used in the configuration of a phrase, it will be a multiple-core phrase. The following piece from Iranian traditional music is an example of a piece built based on two-core phrases.

In a greater layer of phrasing, we should examine the construction of music sentences and music periods. Every music sentence may come to exist by conjoining two or more music phrases, and every music period is built upon two or three music sentences. In the two-sentence periods, the first music sentence usually ends with a mild cadence in the initial key or moves to a relatively close tonality or mode and ends there. In the three-sentence periods, we encounter another type of musical balance. The three-sentence periods are usually in "vocal form" where the third sentence is usually a simple or modified repetition of the first sentence.

"Articulation" is an important tool in the hands of the musician to draw and emphasise musical phrasing. Articulation in music involves how a performer executes various elements, like timing, accents, and pitch transitions. Similar to punctuation in writing, it helps to organise musical phrases, enabling both the musician and the listener to understand the piece's structure.

Articulation can have a significant impact on the overall musical expression, as it can convey different emotions and moods. Articulation in music helps in phrasal distinctions by defining the beginnings and endings of musical phrases. By using different articulation techniques, a musician can create a clear separation between one phrase and the next, making it easier for the listener to follow the structure of the music. For example, a musician might use a strong accent or a staccato articulation to mark the end of a phrase. This will make it clear to the listener that a new phrase is beginning and help them anticipate what is coming next. Similarly, a legato articulation or a smooth transition between notes can help to connect phrases and create a sense of continuity.

Articulation can also be used to highlight important moments in the music, such as the climax of a piece or a particularly expressive melody. By using a strong articulation or a change in articulation technique, the musician can draw attention to these moments and create a sense of drama or emotion.

Articulation gives unique characteristics to the music of every culture. In Japanese music, for instance, articulation plays an important role in delivering emotion and shaping musical phrases. Different instruments and vocal styles use various techniques to articulate notes and phrases, such as hard and soft attacks, slides, and vibrato. For example, in performing koto, the player uses the fingernails to pluck the strings in a precise and delicate manner to create a distinct sound that is crisp and clear. Similarly, in performing shakuhachi, the player uses a variety of articulation techniques, such as bending notes, to create a unique and expressive sound.

In Hindustani classical music, the human voice is considered to be the primary instrument. Vocalists benefit from a grate range of articulation techniques, including *meend*, *gamak*, and *murki*. These techniques enable singers to create intricate melodies and add emotional depth to their performances. The instruments such as the sitar and sarod also use various ornamentation techniques some of which are shared with vocal ornamentations. Here are a number of commonly used ornamentation techniques in sitar performance:

1. *Meend*: This technique involves sliding from one note to another, often used for creating a smooth and flowing sound.
2. *Gamak* (*Gamaka*): This technique involves oscillating between two or more notes in quick succession, creating a vibrant and lively sound.
3. *Murki*: This technique involves playing a quick and subtle sequence of notes, often used to add embellishment and ornamentation to a melody.
4. *Krintan*: This technique involves playing a short, sharp note or sequence of notes, often used to add emphasis or contrast to a melody.
5. *Tan*: This technique involves playing a fast sequence of notes in a particular scale, often used for creating excitement and energy in a performance.

Ornamentations are an essential part of a musical culture's identity and contribute to its unique sound and style. They are not necessarily presented in written music, and the only way of acquiring their essence is through real music performances.

Harmonic Structure

Harmonic structure can be used to create a variety of emotional responses in the listener. Harmonic structure helps musicians to create music that is both emotionally engaging and musically interesting. The harmonic structure is a powerful tool for creating identity in a musical culture. Using certain chords, chord progressions and harmonic settings can give a sense or convey

- A certain time and place
- A particular musical genre
- Various emotional senses
- Telling folk and traditional stories
- Social connectivity and community

Sensing a Particular Time and Place

The harmonic structure tells us when and where we are. Certain chords or chord progressions can be associated with a particular region or country in a particular era. The complexity of harmony in Western musical culture led to certain rules and conventions of chord progression and modulations which have evolved over time. The rise of the modern period in Western music influenced harmonic structure more than any other musical elements. It is known as the "20th century harmony" and is greatly different from the harmonic structure of its previous time known as "tonal harmony" which had emerged in the 17th century and reached its peak in the 19th century. The 20th-century harmony challenged tonal harmony and benefits from atonality, serialism, polytonality, microtonality, and machinery noises.

The harmonic structure of a piece of music that is meant to represent Southern America may use a lot of blues and jazz influences, while the harmonic structure of a piece of music that is meant to represent the Middle East may use a lot of Arabic, Persian, and Turkish influences. In Indian classical music, the harmonic framework is centred around ragas, which imbues the music with a spiritual and mystical quality.

Expressing a Particular Musical Genre

One of the major differences between classical music and popular music is the progression of chords and harmonic configuration. In pre-composed musical genres such as symphonies, the composer spends a great deal of time precisely setting the harmonic duty of every instrument, every part, and every section, while in improvised-based genres such as jazz, the chord progression takes place in moments and very much depends on the current senses and emotion of the performers. Most folk songs give less attention to harmony while trying to pay attention to the linear musical substances, such as melody, rhythm and lyrics.

Conveying Emotional Senses

The harmonic structure of a piece of music can be used to evoke a particular emotion or mood, such as joy, sadness, or anger. It is believed the harmonic structure of a piece of sad music may use a lot of minor chords, while the harmonic structure of a piece of happy music may use a lot of major chords. Dissonant chords and unresolved harmonies typically give the listener a wide variety of emotions and sensations, including instability, uneasiness, excitement, surprise, intensity, and a need or resolution, while consonant harmonies are often associated with positive emotions, such as happiness, peace, and tranquility. They can also create a sense of stability and security.

Telling Stories

Stories play a significant role in shaping the cultural identity of every society. It is believed that harmony aids storytelling. The harmonic structure of a song can be used to create a sense of narrative, with the different chords and chord progressions representing different events in the story. This is often seen in religious music, where the harmonic structure of a hymn can be used to tell the story of a biblical event or to convey a moral message. Here are some examples of how harmony is used in telling stories in music:

- Represent different characters or emotions: (e.g., using dissonant harmonies to represent a villain or a scary scene, while using consonant harmonies to represent a hero or a happy scene.)
- Creating a sense of tension or suspense: (e.g., using a series of dissonant chords to build up tension before resolving to a consonant chord, which can create a sense of relief or satisfaction for the listener.)
- Generating a sense of movement or progression: (e.g., a series of chords that move in a particular direction, such as from tonic to dominant to subdominant, might create a sense of forward momentum.)
- Building a special atmosphere or mood: (e.g., using slow, low chords to create a sense of sadness or melancholy, while using fast, high chords to create a sense of excitement or joy.)

Sense of Social Connectivity and Community

A harmonic structure can give a sense of social connectivity and community. The shared experience of the harmonic setting of music is the most important issue in this regard. Certain harmonic structures can evoke emotions that are associated with social interaction. For instance, the chords set on perfect fourth in *the dastgāhi* musical system evoke social connections for Persian listeners. While minor chords, which evoke sad emotions for Western listeners, can create a sense of empathy and understanding. This sense of empathy helps to build bonds between people.

A certain harmonic structure that is used in a specific ceremony or ritual has similar social functions for people of that society. It includes ceremonies of rites of passage like weddings, births, and funerals, religious services, political rallies, and political movements like protests.

Texture and Vertical Relations

The way that different musical lines are combined plays a significant role in shaping the sound and mood of a composition, resulting in a diverse range of effects. Musical texture is an interplay between different musical elements, such as melody, harmony, rhythm, dynamics, and orchestration, and how they interact with each other vertically. The musical texture of a particular culture can provide insight into the cultural values, beliefs, and practices that have shaped the development of that musical tradition.

The different musical cultures and eras have developed unique approaches to shaping the texture over time. Therefore, every musical texture can indicate the time period of a particular musical culture, too.

The texture of a piece of music can be changed in a number of ways, such as by adding or removing instruments, changing the tempo, or changing the dynamics. Texture can also be used to create contrast within a piece of music.

In Western art music, texture is typically defined by the way different melodic lines combine. However, it may be defined differently in various music cultures. In African music, for instance, it mostly refers to the way various lines rhythmically and metrically combine together.

Different musical cultures have different preferences for musical texture. In Western classical music, polyphony is often used to create a sense of complexity and sophistication. While in Indian classical music, we witness both monophony to create a sense of simplicity and purity and heterophony for excitement. In African music, polymeric and heterophonic melodies are often used to create a sense of excitement and energy. For example, a call and response is a type of heterophonic music that is characterised by its use of two or more voices that sing the same melody, but with slight variations. Call and response is also used in many other cultures in an entirely different way. In the United States, the blues is a genre of music that is characterised by its use of a call-and-response texture. This texture is created when a singer sings a line and then a group of musicians responds with a short phrase.

It is a misleading concept that one relates one musical texture to one musical culture. A musical culture may have a variety of musical genres each of which contain various textures. In Japanese music, for instance, monophony is often used in folk music, such as in the *shakuhachi* music of *Zen* Buddhism. Homophony is often used in Japanese classical music, such as in the *gagaku* music of the imperial court. Polyphony is less common, but it can be found in some genres, such as in the *Noh* theatre music. Heterophony is common in several Japanese countryside folk music, such as in the *minyo*. The texture of Japanese music is also influenced by the instruments that are used. For example, the *shakuhachi* is a solo instrument that is often used to create a monophonic texture. The *koto* is a stringed instrument that is often used to create a homophonic texture. The shamisen is a stringed instrument that is often used to create a heterophonic texture.

Understanding the different textures used in different musical cultures gives a better appreciation of the music of those cultures.

Instrumentations

Instrumentation plays a central role in giving identity to different musical cultures. The choice of instruments used in a particular style of music can create a distinct sound that sets it apart from other styles. For example, the *sitār* and *tablā* are iconic instruments in Indian classical music. Their unique timbres and intricate rhythms are synonymous with this tradition. Similarly, the use of the *tār, ūd*, *ney*, and *darbūkā* are essential to creating the distinctive sound of Middle Eastern music. In contrast, the use of acoustic string instruments, such as the guitar, double bass, fiddle, banjo, mandolin, steel guitar, and Dobro creates the distinct sound of bluegrass music.

Chorshanbe Goibnazarov reports the place of a central Asian musical instrument called the Rabbab in shaping the cultural identity of Muslims in Pamir.

> After the breakdown of the Soviet system, the Rabbob re-emerged, and modified versions of the instrument were produced. Though still fashioned in the old form and retaining aspects of the old playing techniques, the instrument makers now utilize different religious and nationalist decorative patterns on the instruments. In its basic form, each part of the instrument is ascribed a sacred meaning metaphorically assigned to the physical and spiritual worlds, thus acquiring special status in the cultural and national schemes. The instrument, through its function in the music culture, as well as its place in the social and cultural life of the Pamiri Ismailis, expresses various identities of and to the people.
>
> (Goibnazarov, 2017, p. 5)

In Greek traditional dance music, *Bouzouki* and *Tzoura* play significant roles. They are typically accompanied by the *Toubeleki* or the *Daouli*. These instruments help to provide the rhythm and groove for the music, allowing the Bouzouki or/and *Tzoura* to take on a lead role in the melody. Together, these instruments create a vibrant and dynamic sound that is characteristic of Greek traditional music.

Instrumentation can indicate the historical period of a piece of music in its culture in a number of ways, including

- Type of instruments
- Techniques of performance
- Status and function of instruments within the orchestras and ensembles
- Size and composition of the ensemble
- Cultural and social context

Type of Instruments

Different types of instruments were invented and developed at different times in history. For example, the piano was invented in the 18th century, so a piece of music that features a piano is likely from that time period or later. Some instruments became more popular and others lost their popularity. For instance, Persian harps were the most popular instrument from 3000 B.C.E. until the 17th century, but they lost their popularity thereafter.

Techniques of Performance

The techniques and the methods of playing instruments can evolve with time. For instance, the Russian banjo or balalaika progressed over time. Initially, it was played in a traditional folk style, which included strumming, plucking, and some fingerpicking. Over time, musicians started to experiment with new techniques, such as tremolo and staccato, which created a more dynamic sound. In the 20th century, the banjo began to be incorporated into genres like jazz and rock, leading to the introduction of new techniques like tapping and palm muting for unique sounds. Along with these new styles, musicians began to use new playing techniques, such as tapping and palm muting, to create unique sounds and textures. Today, it is played using a wide range of techniques, from traditional strumming and plucking to modern tapping and fingerstyle techniques. These diverse approaches have helped to keep the instrument relevant and popular with musicians of all genres.

Status and Function of Instruments Within the Orchestras and Ensembles

By considering the availability, status, and function of instruments, it is possible to gain insights into the time period of a musical culture. For example, the modern symphony orchestra developed in the 18th century, and it includes instruments that were not used in earlier ensembles, such as the piano, the harp, and the trombone. The use of these new instruments helped to create a new sound that was associated with the modern era. Moreover, the relative importance of different instruments can change over time. For example, in the Baroque era, the harpsichord was the most important instrument in the orchestra. In the classical era, however, the violin became the most important instrument. This change in the status of different instruments helped to create a new sound that was associated with the classical era.

In addition to changing the status of instruments in different periods, the function of different instruments and the way that instruments are combined can also change over time. The use of lead guitar, rhythm guitar, bass guitar, and drums are essential components of rock music. However, in the earliest rock and roll styles, either the piano or saxophone was typically the lead instrument. These instruments were generally replaced or supplemented by guitars in the middle to late 1950s. We can see similar developments in Spanish music, too. In the early days of Spanish music, the most common instruments were the human voice, drums, and simple string instruments. As Spanish culture developed, new instruments were introduced, such as the guitar, the harp, and the flute. In the 19th century, the piano became popular in Spain, and it began to be used in a variety of musical genres. In the 20th century, new musical styles, such as flamenco and jazz, influenced the instrumentation of Spanish music.

Size and Composition of the Ensemble

The size and composition of the ensemble can also change over time. A piece of music that is written for a large orchestra is likely from a later time period than a piece of music that is written for a small chamber ensemble. For instance, in ancient China, ensembles were typically small, consisting of just a few instruments because music was often performed in private settings and musical instruments were expensive. In the Song dynasty (960–1279) China began to develop. It led to enlarging the size of ensembles. In this period musical instruments became more available and public music performances became popular. By the Ming dynasty (1368–1644), the size of ensembles again expanded. This trend continued in the Qing dynasty (1644–1912) when large ensembles were used to perform for the imperial court. In the 20th century, Chinese music underwent a period of rapid change. Western musical influences began to be incorporated into Chinese music, and new genres of music, such as popular music and film music emerged.

Symbolic Characteristics of Instruments in Cultural and Social Context

In addition to the structural elements of instrumentation in the music formation of every culture, the outlook of indigenous people toward the instruments plays a significant role in the musical identity of every culture. The instruments that are used in indigenous music are often made from natural materials and are believed to have spiritual powers. This connection to nature is important for many indigenous cultures, as they believe that humans are part of the natural world, not separate from it. The instrumentation of Tibetan music, for instance, is often used to create a sense of spirituality and mysticism. The use of the human voice, wind instruments, and percussion instruments can create a sense of grandeur and majesty, while the use of string instruments can create a sense of melody and harmony. The overall effect is often one of peace, tranquillity, and spiritual enlightenment. Musical instruments often comprise certain symbolic characteristics in different cultures. Moreover, the choice of instruments used in a particular style of music and a particular period of time helps composers to soundly represent various cultures in different eras. To exemplify this I provide some examples from various musical cultures here.

Didgeridoo in Australia

The *didgeridoo*, which is a wind instrument, has a crucial place among Aboriginal Australians. It is believed to have been created by the Rainbow Serpent, a creator deity in Aboriginal mythology. The *didgeridoo* is used in a variety of ceremonies and rituals, and it is believed to have the power to heal, protect, and connect people to the land. It is often played during Dreamtime ceremonies, which hold significant spiritual importance for Aboriginal peoples. These ceremonies are believed to invoke ancestral spirits and create harmony between humans and nature (Moonstone, 2024). The didgeridoo has also become a popular instrument for meditation and relaxation. Its rhythmic and hypnotic sounds are believed to promote mindfulness, reduce stress, and enhance creativity. The instrument's ability to induce a state of deep relaxation has made it a valuable tool for therapeutic purposes (Australian wnzlnc, 2024).

Djembe Drum in West Africa

The djembe drum is imbued with profound symbolic significance within African culture, serving as a vital conduit for spiritual connection, community bonding, and cultural identity. "Traditionally the djembe is perceived as a cultural practice surrounded by and infused with ancient symbolism, and used primarily as a means of communication between different tribal villages and as an accompaniment to ritualistic tribal ceremonies" Cooke (2017, p. 89). In rituals and ceremonies, the djembe facilitates communion with ancestral spirits, allowing participants to experience a deep sense of unity and belonging. It symbolises joy and celebration, often featured in festivities that strengthen social ties within communities. Moreover, djembe's rhythmic beats serve as a form of expression, telling stories and conveying emotions that resonate with the human experience while promoting healing and spiritual wellbeing.

Scottish Bagpipes

Bagpipes are deeply associated with Scottish culture and identity. They symbolise national pride and heritage, often played at celebrations, memorials, and events to evoke a sense of belonging and remembrance.

> In Scottish weddings, bagpipes hold a special and revered place, adding a sense of tradition and grandeur to the celebration. During the ceremony, the bagpipes might be used to punctuate key moments, such as the signing of the marriage register or the exchange of vows.
>
> (Levine, 2025)

Historically, bagpipes have been associated with Scottish regiments and have served as motivational tools in warfare. "Army Pipe Bands developed around the mid-1800s, when regimental pipers and drummers would play together on long route marches in order to keep a steady tempo and maintain the morale of the troops" (Small, 2016). The role of pipers on the battlefield exemplifies their significance in maintaining morale and fostering a sense of camaraderie among soldiers, further entrenching their status as instruments of honour and bravery in the face of adversity.

Peruvian Cajón

The cajón is a box-shaped percussion instrument. Its origins trace back to the mid-18th century when African slaves in coastal Peru. The cajón is often used in celebrations and is a vital part of traditional music genres like festejo and landó. "Celebrations such as the Corpus Christi Festival[12] in Cusco highlight the fusion of indigenous and Spanish colonial influences, where traditional music, often accompanied by the cajón, plays a vital role in the processions of saints" (FWTP, 2025). The cajón has transcended its traditional boundaries, integrating into various modern music genres, from jazz to pop.

Chinese Pipa

The pipa is a traditional Chinese lute that symbolises elegance and cultural refinement. It is often linked to classical Chinese literature and art, embodying the pursuit of beauty and artistic expression. As noted by Myers (1992),

> Pipa music has been cherished by the Chinese people for centuries. During the Ming (1368–1644) and Qing (1645–1911) dynasties, several pipa schools emerged in the South, particularly in Wuxi, Suzhou, and Shanghai, as well as in the North, especially in Beijing, each showcasing distinct styles.

The pipa's versatility is evident in its role across various Chinese music genres, including folk music, opera, and contemporary compositions. Its ability to transition seamlessly between these styles underscores its adaptability, allowing the instrument to enrich both traditional and modern musical landscapes while capturing the essence of different eras and expressions.

Persian Ney

The Persian Ney which is a traditional reed flute symbolises the deep emotional and spiritual connection to Persian culture and poetry. It is often associated with themes of longing and love, the pain of separation and the quest for divine union. The Ney serves as a bridge between the earthly and the mystical and highlights the importance of music as a means of communication and reflection in Iranian society.

Overall Formal Structure

The overall formal structure of a piece of music refers to the way that the different parts of the piece are arranged. The overall formation of a piece plays a significant role in the listener's experience. For example, a piece of music with a straightforward and anticipated structure can be easier to follow and understand, while a piece of music with a more complex or unpredictable structure can be more challenging and engaging.

Micro-analysis vs. Macro-analysis

There are two general views in structural analysis: micro-analysis and macro-analysis. A view in which the details of musical components, such as intervals, melodic contours, chord progressions, and so on are analysed is called micro-analysis. Analysis of the overall formal structure in music and the way that a piece of music is organised is macro-analysis. This can include the order of the sections, the length of the sections, and the way that the sections are related to each other. The overall formal structure provides a framework for the piece, while the music components provide the details. The two work together to create a sense of unity and coherence, as well as to create a variety of moods and emotions.

There are many different types of formal structures, and each one can create a different effect. In a broad view, we can consider two kinds of musical forms: "sectional" or part forms and "continuous" forms. Sectional or part-form is a type of musical form in which the music is divided into distinct sections. Pieces in part forms have clear phrases and periods. Each section is usually based on a different melody, harmony, and rhythm. Some common types of formal structure in Western music include strophic, binary, ternary, rondo, theme and variations, and through-composed. The sectional form is often used in folk songs, hymns, and children's songs.

Continuous form, on the other hand, is a type of musical form in which the music flows from one section to the next without any breaks. Continuous form is often used in classical music, jazz, and rock music. The main difference between the continuous structure and the part forms is that the phrases and parts in continuous forms are less clear. The continuous forms in Western art music are limited to a passacaglia, canon, round, ricercare, fugue, and a few other imitative forms.

The Overall Structure of the Loops

One of the most common techniques employed in game design is the use of looping music tracks. This approach allows a piece of music to repeat seamlessly until a specific event or trigger occurs within the game. A game may feature a single loop that encompasses the entire round, or it could involve multiple loops activated by the player, depending on the level of attention it draws.

Creating music that loops effectively presents a unique set of challenges. One of the primary concerns is ensuring that the repetition does not become monotonous. Composers might create variations in the arrangement, such as introducing subtle changes in instrumentation or dynamics as the loop progresses. This technique can help maintain the player's interest over time, making the music feel fresh even after multiple repetitions. Additionally, some games incorporate interactive elements, where the music responds to player actions or changes in the game environment. Another factor to consider is when the loop transitions to a different piece or ends altogether. This transition is critical, as it should feel natural and enhance the narrative or gameplay experience.

If the loop is too short or lacks variety, players may quickly grow weary of hearing the same melody or rhythm, which can detract from their overall enjoyment of the game. To mitigate the risk of annoying players with repetitions, composers often employ several strategies. Guy Michelmore (2021, p. 68) summarises the musical aspects involved in creating loops as follows:

- Harmonic structure, to avoid awkward harmonic shifts when the loop repeats. Many looped cues use a cadence to connect the end of the loop back to the beginning.
- Timbres and textures so that musical statements and reverb are not noticeably cut off when the loop repeats.
- Melodic material, which must avoid listener fatigue. Winifred Phillips suggests using continual variation to mitigate this issue.
- Dynamic and rhythmic progression during the cue so that when the loop returns to the start, it does not sound like a lowering of musical tension, which may not match with in-game action.
- Ending the loop or transitioning to another musical section. How will the loop end in a way that is musically satisfying? Should the loop be interrupted, or will the reaction have to wait until the loop concludes? Will a transition passage or crossfade be required?

The Overall Structure of the Performance Event

At a greater layer of the overall formal structure of a piece, we may consider the shape and order of the pieces which are performed in an event of music performance. Music is an inseparable part of rituals and traditional festivals. The order of the musical pieces played during a ceremony is often carefully planned to create a specific mood or atmosphere.

The nature of the pieces and the order of their performances are set by the traditional conventions, and they are unique to that society. For instance, in a typical wedding ceremony in Pakistan, songs are used to mark different points of the ceremony, such as the *mehndi*, *barāt,* and *walima*. The *mehndi* ceremony is a pre-wedding celebration, where the bride's hands and feet are decorated with henna. The music played at this event is typically festive, and it often includes traditional Punjabi folk songs. The *barāt* is the procession of the groom and his family to the bride's home for the wedding ceremony. The music played at this event is typically more traditional and formal, and it often includes Sufi devotional songs such as *qawwali*. The *walima* is the wedding reception, which is held after the *nikah*, or marriage formal ceremony of setting and signing a marriage contract usually done by religious clergy. The music played at this event is typically more festive, and it often includes popular Pakistani pop songs.

Each point of ceremonies related to the rite of passage is usually marked by a certain song or music. In Tibet, for instance, each point of a funeral ceremony is marked by a distinct song. The first song is often a prayer for the deceased, asking for their soul to be guided to a good rebirth. The second song is about the deceased's life, their accomplishments, and their loved ones. The third song describes the afterlife. The fourth song tries to bring back hope and renewal and offer comfort to the mourners. In addition to these four songs, there may also be other songs that are played during the funeral, such as traditional Tibetan folk songs or songs that were special to the deceased.

Stage traditional music in many cultures follows a planned order of the pieces one after another from opening to the end among them are Arabic *maqāmi* music, Persian and Azeri *dastgāhi* music, Indian *rāga* music, and so on. In Indian music, for instance, four main sections are performed in order, including *alāp*, *jhor*, *jhala*, and *gat*. The order of the sections in a performance can vary, but the *alāp* is usually the first section, and the *gat* is usually the last section. The *jhor* and *jhala* can be placed anywhere in the performance, depending on the mood and atmosphere that the musician wants to create. The overall plan of a performance event is one of the characteristics of the musical identity of every culture.

Lyrical Structure

Songs, both in content and structure, reflect the cultural, social, and political context in which they were created, and can provide insight into the values, beliefs, and struggles of a particular community or culture. Songs can serve as powerful tools for transmitting cultural knowledge and preserving cultural traditions across generations. To investigate the function of lyrics in shaping the construction of musical identity, we have to look at various issues including

- The use of language
- The use of imagery
- The use of symbolism
- The use of themes
- The use of musical elements
- The overall mood and atmosphere

The Use of Language

An entire chapter has been dedicated to the topic of language in this book, and I am not going to repeat the issues raised in that chapter here. The language structure of the lyric has a major impact on shaping the musical configuration, even in instrumental music. Quantitative languages like Arabic, Persian, and Greek mostly influence the durational patterns of rhythmic structure, and qualitative languages which are built based on stress differentiations have a great impact in shaping pulsations and configuring metric structure. The tonal languages may influence the tone setting of the songs as well as their melodic contour (to see more on the impact of language structure on shaping music refer to the chapter on language).

The Use of Imagery

Imagery refers to the use of language and sensory details to create vivid pictures in the mind and sensational emotional responses in the listener. By using imagery that is specific to a particular culture or community, songwriters can create a strong sense of cultural identity and help convey the values, beliefs, and experiences of that culture. Songwriters have the ability to weave a complex web of emotions and insights that expand our insight into the diversity of human experiences. Jan Assmann (1995) makes a distinction between "communicative" and "cultural memory." He posits that cultural memory provides a framework for groups to maintain their identity across generations through shared knowledge and rituals, contrasting it with the more ephemeral nature of communicative memory, which is rooted in everyday interactions and has a limited temporal scope. He highlights how cultural memory, characterised by its objectivised forms – such as texts, rites, and monuments – serves as a stabilising force for group identity, offering fixed points that transcend time. Assmann's analysis suggests that the structural qualities of cultural memory allow for the preservation and evolution of collective narratives through generations, making it a significant element in the understanding of poetry and its imagery as a reflection of shared cultural experiences.

Imagery from the natural world, including animals, plants, and landscapes, is frequently incorporated into the music of indigenous communities to underscore their strong bonds with the environment and to convey their spiritual and cultural traditions. For example, in the folk songs of Appalachia, imagery related to the natural world, such as mountains, rivers, and forests, is often used to create a sense of connection to the land and a rural way of life. In Greek songs, too, poetic imagery mostly comprises nature and love.

> Imagery is neither merely decorative nor does it offer a pictorial representation of the natural world. Frequently the architectonic patterns of a song or the progress of a theme are worked out in terms of images, and these images often invoke the natural world as a reflection of human emotions or attributes, and also perhaps as an arbiter of order.
>
> (Beaton, 1980, p. 58)

A number of the most common poetic imagery in Greek traditional and folk songs are presented here:

The use of imagery in poetry evolves over time, reflecting changes in society, culture, and artistic trends. In the Greek case, for instance, poetic imagery was often used to celebrate the gods, goddesses, nature, and heroic deeds in ancient times. During the Byzantine era, Greek music and poetry became more religious in nature, with imagery focused on divine and spiritual themes. This imagery was often highly ornate and stylised, with a focus

The sea	The sea is a recurring motif in Greek songs, symbolising both the vastness of the world and the emotions that it evokes. The sea is often depicted as a place of escape and freedom, as well as a source of danger and uncertainty.
The sun	The sun represents warmth, light, and hope. It is often used to convey a sense of optimism and joy, as well as a reminder of the passing of time.
Nature	Greek songs frequently draw on the natural world for their imagery, with references to flowers, trees, animals, and landscapes. These images are used to evoke a sense of beauty and wonder, as well as to reflect on the cycles of life and death.
Love	Love is a central theme in many Greek songs, and its imagery can range from the romantic to the tragic. Love is often depicted as a powerful force that can bring both joy and pain, and its imagery may include references to hearts, roses, and other symbols of passion.
War	Greek songs frequently draw on imagery related to war and struggle, reflecting the country's history of conflict and resistance. This imagery may include references to weapons, battles, and heroes, as well as symbols of sacrifice and perseverance.

La Rosa	The rose is a symbol of love and passion in Spanish songs. It is often used to represent the beauty and intensity of romantic relationships.
El Sol	The sun is a symbol of warmth, hope, and energy in Spanish songs. It is often used to represent the power and vitality of life.
La Luna	The moon is a symbol of mystery, beauty, and femininity in Spanish songs. It is often used to represent the emotional depth and complexity of human experience.
La Guitarra	The guitar is a symbol of Spanish music and culture. It is often used to represent the power and passion of music.
El Mar	The sea is a symbol of adventure, freedom, and possibility in Spanish songs. It is often used to represent the vastness and wonder of the natural world.
La Tierra	The earth is a symbol of sustenance, connection, and belonging in Spanish songs. It is often used to represent the importance of family, community, and cultural heritage.

on the beauty and grandeur of the divine. In the modern era, Greek songs have become more diverse and eclectic, drawing on a range of influences from both within and outside of Greece. In spite of that, many modern Greek songs still draw on traditional imagery related to love, nature, and the sea, but they also explore a range of new themes and symbols, such as urban life, social issues, and global concerns.

The Use of Symbolism

Symbols are objects, images, or actions that represent something beyond their literal meaning, often carrying emotional, spiritual, or cultural significance. By using symbols that are familiar and meaningful to a particular culture, songwriters can create a sense of connection and solidarity among listeners who share that cultural background. For example, in traditional Irish music, symbols such as the shamrock, the Claddagh ring, and the harp are used to evoke a sense of pride in Irish cultural heritage and identity. The Spanish songs contain certain symbols which give a unique identity to music. Follows are a number of examples of Spanish poetic symbols used in traditional and folk songs (Masera, 2019):

Each symbol carries its own unique meaning and significance, helping to create a rich sense of cultural identity and artistic expression.

The Use of Themes

There are themes that are popular in nearly all cultures like love, separation, and reunion. Nonetheless, certain themes are specifically popular in definite cultures. For example, many songs in the African-American blues tradition explore themes of struggle, loss, and oppression, reflecting the experiences of Black Americans throughout history. Similarly, many songs in the Native American tradition are rooted in the land and the natural world, reflecting the profound connection that Native communities have to their environment. The lamentations of losses and disasters are also another main theme of Indian Americans. A very moving and sympathetic lament for the vanishing race comes in the form of James G. Clark's "The Indian Mother's Lullaby" (1855). In the first verse, Clark sets the scene in a wilderness where the mother comforts her child. We hear the stages of the tribe's defeat in the remaining verses (quoted in Finson, 1997, p. 249):

> Sleep, while gleams the council fire
> Kindled by thy hunted sire;
> Guarded by thy God above,
> Sleep and dream of peace and love.

These themes not only serve as a reflection of individual and collective experiences but also act as a means of cultural expression. Through folk songs, people convey deep emotional truths that resonate across generations, fostering a sense of identity and continuity. The exploration of such themes reveals the shared human experiences that connect us all, while also honouring the unique narratives that shape specific cultures.

The Use of Musical Elements

There is a two-way connection between poetry and music. Poetry is one of the components of a song, while music is one of the constituent elements of poetry that has a significant impact on the overall sound and meaning of a song. Songwriters incorporate musical elements such as rhythm, rhyme, and melody into the lyrics to create a cohesive and compelling musical experience for the listener.

The musical elements of poems work mainly in three different scopes: rhythmic structure, consistency of materials, and inner coherence. The rhythmic and metric configurations come to exist through poetic feet. The rhyme of the final words of the lines and stanzas provides consistency of material. The verbal music formations and semantic proportions provide the inner musical entity of lines.

Rhythmic structure: The rhythmic and metric configuration of poems is often structured by poetic feet. A poetic foot refers to a unit of meter that consists of a pattern of contrasted syllables. In qualitative languages like German and English, the contrast comes to exist through stressed and unstressed syllables. The four common poetic feet in English poetry are listed below (the stressed syllables are marked by capital letters):

Foot	*Pattern*	*Example*
iamb	U –	aLONE
trochee	– U	ONly
anapest	UU –	in a DREAM
dactyl	– UU	MEmories

By using these different poetic feet in combination, poets can create complex and varied rhythmic patterns that help to give their poems a unique and distinctive sound. For example, a poem composed entirely of iambs will have a consistent, steady rhythm, while a poem that incorporates a variety of different poetic feet will have a more dynamic and varied rhythm. In addition to creating rhythmic patterns, the use of poetic feet can also help to create emphasis and meaning within a poem. By placing stress on certain words or phrases, poets can create a sense of importance or significance, drawing attention to certain ideas or themes within the poem.

In quantitative languages like Persian, Arabic, Greek . . . the poetic feet are configured based on contrasted durational settings of syllables (to see differences between qualitative and quantitative musical structure refer to the chapter on language).

The Overall Mood and Atmosphere

The mood and atmosphere in a song is a sum of all poetic and musical elements on one hand and the environmental and cultural context on the other. Once a certain genre of music is associated with specific poetic imagery, symbols played in a specific cultural context will bring a unique experience to its listeners. The visual and surrounding elements of a performance, such as lighting, costumes, and stage design, can also contribute to the mood of a song.

The audience's interaction during a performance significantly influences the mood of a song. Therefore, game designers who incorporate opportunities for players to engage with music can greatly enhance the emotional impact of a song. If the audience is actively participating, dancing, or singing along, it can create an energetic and celebratory mood. Alan Lomax (1962) uses social participation in performance as one of the bases of the classification scheme in his *cantometrics*. In *cantometrics*, Lomax suggests a system of measurement to study qualitative aspects of man's musical behaviour within society. A set of features including the size and social structure of the music-making group; the location and role of leadership in the music-making group; the type and the degree of integration in the music-making group; the type and the degree of melodic, rhythmic, and vocal embellishment in a sung performance; and the qualities of singing voice normally effected by the chosen singers in a culture (Lomax, 1962, p. 427). From this perspective, Alan Lomax describes American Indian songs as follows:

> Among the Fox Indians individuals were trained from childhood to venture reliantly into the wilderness. Collective activity was at a minimum, and, when it occurred, it was unforced, each individual participating, not upon command, but because he knew from tradition what he should do and how and when he should do it. Just as the individual Indian might ask for and obtain power directly from a supernatural source, so he might acquire a medicine song from the spirit world that would give him the power to heal or to lead a war party. The shape of the American Indian musical group conforms to the pattern of role-taking. The solo singer uses a chesty voice, wide rather than narrow, yet with strong characterisers of nasal resonance and throaty burr and with forceful accents a voice which is expressive of a full-blown and unrepressed masculinity or, perhaps better, of a strong bodily orientation.
>
> The leader initiates the song but then is submerged in a chorus performing the same musical material in unison. This chorus links their bassy, resonant voices with moderate tonal blending but in a precise rhythmic concert. Individual voices in these choruses can still be heard, and the effect is of a loosely knit but well-coordinated group of individuals cooperating in relation to a common goal.
>
> (Lomax, 1962, p. 446)

The setting in which a song is performed can also greatly impact the mood. A performance in a formal concert hall comprises an entirely different mood compared to a performance in a local teahouse.

> In Afghanistan, live music finds a secure niche in the teahouse (*chaixana*), where men, who make up the entire body of shoppers, gather for relaxation and gossip. A space is cleared in the corner for the standard teahouse band, which consists of a lead lute player (*damburachi*) and a pair of singers at the minimum. All the performers, like the customers, come from the same belt of satellite villages.
>
> (Slobin, 1970, p. 471)

The nature of the audience like age, gender, cultural background, and social status, may even modify the repertory and the senses of performance in a music event. In Salvador, a Brazilian municipality, performers perform in bars and restaurants commonly referred to as "*músicos da noite*" or "night musicians." In comparison to performers who do "shows," events that might be called concerts in the United States, night musicians are often treated by patrons and employers as part of the atmosphere of a venue and as such are rarely considered "artists." While the venues in which they work do typically provide some means of separating them from patrons, for example, small stages, PA systems, lights, and the like, most *músicos da noite* present their music in a relatively casual manner that makes it possible but not obligatory for audience members to sing along (Packman, 2010, p. 244). There are several other musical cultures that involve casual and interactive performances such as Irish folk songs; Caribbean music including genres like reggae, calypso, and soca; American folk music, including genres like bluegrass and country; and several African and Latin American genres.

Examples presented in this section showed some musical genres are capable of audience participation while others have less capacity for interaction between performers and audiences. In addition to the potential for the participation of gamers, designers should also consider the accessibility and familiarity of the musical genres they choose. If players are already acquainted with a particular style or have positive associations with it, they are likely to engage more deeply with the game.

Notes

1 Drones are long and sustained sounds, heard simultaneously and continuously with the main melody. It is comparable to bass continuous. Drones carry on time without variation and give special atmosphere to the performance.
2 To read more on this issue refer to the other book of the author *Melodic Structure in Iranian Music* published in Persian language by Markaz, Tehran.
3 *Dastgāh (plural: dastgāh-ha):* a modal system in Iranian and Azeri music; a collection of melodic segments that share common basic pith patterns with its variations called *gūsheh-ha*. At the theoretical stage, the first characteristic feature of a *dastgāh* is the quality of its intervals – some of which do not exist in current Western music – and their specific functions within the scale of each *dastgāh*. A *dastgāh* is more specific than a scale, for any number of *gūsheh-ha* can share a single collection of pitch patterns
4 *Gūsheh* (plural: *gūsheh-ha*): a traditional repertory of melodies, melodic formula, tonal progressions, ornamentations and rhythmic patterns that serve as a model for improvisation; units which comprise each *dastgāh* or *āvāz* in Iranian and Azeri music.
5 *Shūr:* largest *dastgāh* in the set of the seven *dastgāh-ha* in contemporary Iranian music; its primary scale is G A^{koron} $B^{\flat}$ C D $E^{\flat}$ F G
6 آ stands for āqāz (opening tone) ش stands for shāhed (central tone); م stands for motoqayer (alternation tone); ی stands for īst (temporary cadence tone); خ stands for khātemeh (ending tone).
7 Koron: a quarter-tone flattened.
8 If you are interested to apply the above method to Europian folk songs you may refer to the collection provided by Helmuth Schaffrath (1995) *The Essen Folksong Collection in Kern Format*. The collection includes 6,251 songs readily available for melodic and rhythmic analysis.
9 Tombak: Iranian goblet drum. For interpretation of the notation system refer to chapter 5 of book *Rhythmic Structure in Iranian Music.*

10 To see full project refer to the 3rd edition of *Rhythmic Structure in Iranian Music.*
11 "Gestalt" is German for "unified whole"
12 On the first full moon after the Catholic celebration of Corpus Christi (in May or June), around one hundred thousand pilgrims from the towns and communities of Cusco head towards the sanctuary of the Lord of Qoyllurit'i on the snowy peak of Sinakara (*ibid.*).

Chapter 6

Sound Symbols

Introduction

Sound symbolism is the study of the relationship between the sound of a word or musical phrase and its comprehension. This concept posits that certain sounds inherently evoke specific meanings or associations. "The notion of sound symbolism indicates that there is synesthetic associations between sounds and sensory experience" (Sasamoto, 2019, p. 18). Sound symbols play an important role in both music and language, helping to create a sense of identity and meaning within a particular culture or community.

In music, symbolisation refers to the use of musical sounds to represent or evoke specific ideas, emotions, or images. In other words, music represents tonal sources and motions of musical performance through symbolism. Music can convey both static and dynamic entities symbolically. Moreover, music can depict real events and objects by representing their characteristic motions. This can be achieved through various musical elements and techniques, such as rhythms, melodies, dynamics, timbre, texture, and instruments that are closely associated with a particular culture or musical tradition. For example, the sound of a particular instrument like the bagpipe can be associated with Scottish music or the sound of a pentatonic scale may be associated with the sound of East Asian music.

In language, sound symbols can refer to how sounds are used to create meaning within a particular language or dialect. For example, the use of tonal inflections in Chinese languages can change the meaning of a word, while the use of different vowel sounds in English can indicate differences in regional accents. These sound symbols help to create a sense of identity and community within a particular language group, reinforcing the shared experiences and cultural practices that define that community.

Formal equivalence is a basic formal relationship between music and other events, including number, motion, and formal characteristics. Moreover, the thought of the person who composes a line of poem took the comprehension of his word beyond the vocabulary and grammar of that language. "One may have a thorough understanding of the French language, and still not understand a poem by Mallarmé" (Zuckerkandl, 1956, p. 41).

DOI: 10.4324/9781003591399-7

Symbolism based on emotive response can be used to represent physical objects and happenings indirectly by seeking to duplicate the emotions they arouse. Sensory impressions, including auditory and visual sensations, are interpreted as symbols of external events. The representative function of sound is an example of a prototype of all symbolism. Musical symbolism is important to musical experience, including spatial interplay between segments of a performing group and recognition of different instruments. Sensory impressions symbolise an underlying and important reality, with symbols serving to recall the whole and effect representing the cause.

Music is emotional and can evoke feelings and moods that are moulded and patterned by it. It most often symbolises situations and physical manifestations rather than abstract emotions. Chromaticism, scales, melodic patterns, chords, and instruments can all serve as symbols that excite specific feelings and moods. Symbolism based on patterns seems capable of representing not only a wider range of objects and happenings but also of representing ideas themselves. Music can depict real events and objects by representing their characteristic motions. Any form or formal characteristic in music will have an unlimited number of symbolic possibilities.

Intersensory sound symbols refer to the use of sound to evoke or represent experiences from multiple sensory modalities. Musicians often use sound symbols to convey emotions, ideas, or narratives that can be interpreted across different senses. For example, a piece of music may evoke imagery or specific feelings that resonate with visual or tactile experiences. Intersensory symbols are based on elemental attributes of tone, such as pitch, volume, brightness, tone-colour, and loudness. The tonal symbol is based on the brightness of high tones and also on rapidity. Wagner's leitmotifs are effective due to his sensitivity to relations between the senses. Intersensory symbols have been thought out or devised in certain cultural settings and have called forth a similarly detached response. In some African cultures, certain drum patterns or rhythmic movements are used to evoke specific emotions or tell stories from the past.

A symbol directs us to something that we call its meaning, which has some degree of independence from the symbol itself. Any audible occurrence may be imitated, including unlikely objects of musical attention such as the sound of snoring. Imitation is a kind of deceit that presents physical entities and is active only when the composer practices it. One instrument or voice may imitate another, and instrumental imitation of singing is possible. Musical structure can reveal fundamental ways of organising material and fundamental modes of thought.

Sound Symbols and Meanings

Mutsumi Imai and Sotaro Kita (2014) argue against the traditional view of sound symbolism as a marginal phenomenon in language. They propose that sound symbolism plays a crucial role in both language acquisition and evolution, acting as a valuable scaffold for children as they learn to map speech sounds to meanings. Their article highlights how infants and young children exhibit sensitivity to sound-symbolic correspondences, aiding in their ability to establish word-referent associations and extract invariant meanings from complex stimuli. Imai and Kita also suggest that this sensitivity to sound symbolism may reflect a vestige of protolanguage, reinforcing the idea that iconic relationships between sound and meaning are integral to language development.

Leanne Hinton and colleagues (2006) consider a hierarchical linkage between sound symbolisms and their meanings. They propose a scale for representing language utterances based on four types of sound symbolism according to the kinds and directness degree of their meaning. They suggest that one end of the scale reflects utterances influenced by sound symbolism, while the other end represents those shaped by everyday use and social conventions. Here are hierarchical linkage between sound symbolisms and their meanings (after Hinton et al., 2006).

Corporeal sound symbolism ⟷ *Imitative sound symbolism* ⟷ *Synesthetic sound symbolism* ⟷ *Conventional sound symbolism*

1. Corporeal Sound Symbolism

The first type of sound symbolism is called corporeal sound symbolism. Corporeal sound symbolism refers to the way that sounds produced by the body or through vocalisations, whether emotional or physical, can carry meaning and significance in a cultural context. This includes things like coughing, hiccuping, or special tones in the voice. These sounds are closely linked to how the speaker is feeling, making them hard to write down or explain in regular speech.

In some African cultures, there are strong traditions of using sound to express ideas related to the body, emotions, or nature. For instance, in languages like Xhosa and Zulu, certain clicking and consonant sounds have specific meanings tied to physical feelings. Some animal sounds can indeed be considered a form of corporeal sound symbolism among indigenous cultures and their communication practices. For instance, imitating the call of a bird might express joy or alertness, while a low growl might convey danger or displeasure. These sounds are often used in cultural activities like music, stories, and ceremonies.

In video games, expressive voice qualities and intonation patterns can be strategically placed during key narrative moments, allowing players to intuitively grasp the character's feelings without explicit dialogue.

Table 6.1 Expression of emotions in English and Spanish speeches

Language devices	*English*	*Spanish*
Verbs	The verb "to be" expresses our current state of being, including our emotions. For example, we might say "I am happy" or "I am sad."	There are two verbs that can be used to express emotions: "*estar*" and "*ser*." "*Estar*" is used to express temporary emotions, while "*ser*" is used to express more permanent emotions. So, we might say "*Estoy feliz*" (I am happy right now) or "Soy *feliz*" (I am a happy person).
Adjectives	The adjectives used to express emotions in English and Spanish are often different. For example, the English word "happy."	"Happy" is translated as "*feliz*" in Spanish, but there are also other adjectives that can be used to express happiness, such as "*contento*" or "alegre."
Interjections	In English, some common interjections for expressing emotions include "wow," "oops," and "ouch."	In Spanish, some common interjections for expressing emotions include "*¡Ay!*" "*¡Oye!*" and "*¡Caramba!*"
Body language	Eye contact: In English culture, direct eye contact can be seen as aggressive or intimidating.	Eye contact: direct eye contact is seen as a sign of respect and interest.
	Personal space: In English culture, people tend to stand well ahead than in Spanish culture.	Personal space: people tend to stand closer together this is especially true when people are talking to each other.
	Physical contact: In English culture, physical contact is less common than in Spanish culture. It is not common for people to regularly shake hands, hug, or kiss on the cheek when greeting each other.	Physical contact: physical contact is more common. It is not uncommon for people to shake hands, hug, or kiss on the cheek when greeting each other.
	Gestures: English people tend to use fewer gestures than Spanish people when they speak.	Gestures: Spanish people tend to use more gestures than English people when they speak. These gestures can be used to emphasise points, express emotions, or simply to communicate more effectively.
	Facial expressions: English people are less expressive with their facial expressions than Spanish people even when they are talking about emotions.	Facial expressions: Spanish people tend to be more expressive with their facial expressions than English people. This is especially true when they are talking about emotions such as happiness, sadness, or anger.

(*Continued*)

Table 6.1 (Continued)

Language devices	*English*	*Spanish*
Musicality of language	English people tend to have less melodious and expressive intonation, only they may dynamically emphasise on certain syllables. In English, anger is often expressed through a louder and more forceful tone of voice.	Spanish people tend to have a more melodious and expressive intonation, with more variation in pitch and emphasis on certain syllables. This can make Spanish speakers sound more passionate or emotional, even when they are not necessarily feeling strong emotions. In Spanish, anger may be expressed through a faster and more clipped speech pattern.

2. *Imitative Sound Symbolism*

The second category proposed by Hinton is imitative sound symbolism, which involves the words and phrases representing environmental sounds (e.g., bang, bow-wow, swish, knock, etc.). Imitative sound symbolism also includes utterances that utilise sound patterns outside of conventional speech and are difficult to portray in writing, such as representations of bird and animal sounds, etc. It has no direct connection to emotion or physical state, but instead, it has a very important referential role to the objects which it is used to describe.

Oswalt (1994, p. 293) defines imitative sounds as a close representation of non-linguistic noises that have been modified to fit the phonological structure of a specific language. He further categorises imitative expressions into three subtypes for the upcoming analysis: animate, inanimate, and expressive. The distinction between animate and inanimate relates to the source of the imitative sound (for instance, sounds from humans, mammals, or birds versus noises like glass breaking or explosions), while expressive imitations reflect emotional states and attitudes.

Jana Jurčević (2019) highlights the significant role of sound symbolism in linguistic communication, particularly within the context of Croatian vernacular in computer-mediated communication. By analysing chat interactions across various platforms, the research reveals a rich variety of imitative expressions that serve diverse linguistic functions, supporting the hypothesis that sound symbolism aids in maintaining a balance between language economy and system redundancy. Furthermore, the study suggests that the reliance on visual channels in online communication has led to innovative techniques that translate auditory cues into written expressions, enriching the communicative experience. Ultimately, the research positions sound symbolism as a vital and dynamic element of language use in digital contexts, challenging the notion that it is a marginal phenomenon.

Imitative sound symbolism also includes movement imitative. Describing movement imitative, Hinton wrote (Hinton et al., 2006, pp. 3–4):

> Certainly, rhythmic movement often directly produces sound. But beyond that, the rhythms of sound and the rhythms of movement are so closely linked in the human neural system that they are virtually inseparable. This is illustrated in the very natural human physical response to rhythmic music, in the forms of hand clapping, foot tapping, dancing, rhythmic physical labor, etc. Just as humans are capable of translating rhythmic sounds into rhythmic movements, they are also capable of the reverse: translating rhythmic movements into sounds, including sound-symbolic language forms. In the representation of repeated sounds and movements, the linguistic strategy of reduplication is frequently utilised (as in English "ding-dong"), a direct imitation of the rhythm being represented.

Some examples of imitative sound symbolism in various cultures are presented below:

3. *Synesthetic Sound Symbolism*

The third category of sound symbolism is synesthetic sound symbolism. Synaesthesia refers to the phenomenon where a sensation in one sense prompts a perception in another sense. For example, when hearing a specific sound, a person may see a specific colour at the same time. Therefore, synesthetic sound symbolism happens when certain vowels, consonants, and suprasegmentals are chosen to consistently represent visual, tactile, or proprioceptive properties of objects, such as size or shape.

Japanese	The word "pika" is used to describe something shiny or glittering. This sound symbolism imitates the sparkling or twinkling of light.
French	The word "glou-glou" is used to imitate the sound of liquid pouring or being consumed, such as when drinking water or wine.
Russian	The word "тa-тa-тa" is used to imitate the sound of knocking on a door or tapping on a surface.
Mandarin Chinese	The word "gā" is used to imitate the sound of a duck quacking.
English	The word "buzz" is often used to describe the sound of a bee flying or a phone vibrating.
Spanish	The word "tictac" is used to imitate the sound of a clock ticking.
Swahili	The word "mbweha" is used to imitate the sound of a fox yelping.
Arabic	The word "karakar" is used to imitate the sound of a crow cawing.

In the Navajo language, certain words are said to evoke specific visual or sensory experiences. For example, the word "hastiin" is said to evoke the image of a tall, slender man standing upright. In Japanese culture, the word "kiki" is often associated with sharp, angular shapes, while "bouba" is associated with round, smooth shapes. This relationship between sound and shape is a form of synesthetic sound symbolism.

Kaitlyn Bankieris and Julia Simner (2015) explore the intriguing relationship between sound symbolism and synaesthesia. Sound symbolism posits that certain phonological forms can convey semantic meaning in a non-arbitrary manner, as evidenced by studies where participants consistently matched sounds to shapes (e.g., "baluma" to rounded shapes). The authors hypothesise that synaesthetes – individuals who experience heightened cross-sensory integration (e.g., associating sounds with colours) – would demonstrate superior performance in tasks involving sound-symbolic foreign words compared to non-synaesthetes. Their findings show that cultural identity can also be influenced by the interplay of sound symbolism and synaesthesia. They suggest that individuals who experience synesthesia possess an enhanced ability to perceive and interpret the non-arbitrary connections between phonological forms and their semantic meanings. This heightened sensitivity can lead synesthetes to engage with language and cultural symbols in uniquely expressive ways, potentially shaping their personal and communal identities.

4. Conventional Sound Symbolism

Conventional sound symbolism is the fourth category proposed by Hinton. This category is the association of certain phonemes and clusters with certain meanings, for example, the "gl" of glitter, glisten, glow, glimmer, etc. In the English language, the prefixes "in-" and "ex-" are most often used in opposite contexts. The prefix "in-" generally conveys a sense of being within something or indicates negation, lack, or absence. In contrast, "ex-" typically signifies movement out of, removal, or exceeding a limit. Examples of words formed with the prefix "in-" include inside, inhale, include, and internet. Examples of words formed with the prefix "ex-" include exclude, exhale, extract, and exceed.

Moreover, conventional sound symbolism is often language-specific and therefore is closer to the arbitrary end of the language scale. This kind of sound symbolism is generally used when creating names for commercial products or brands such as L'Oréal for shampoo, where the feminine name Laura and the synesthetic sound symbolism for "flowing" sound, symbolising flowing hair, are combined.

Communicating Meaning through Music Symbolism

Symbols are a particular type of sign with a conventional relation between the mark and its meaning. They are used to make meaning by attaching meaning to them in socially contextualised interactive, intersubjective, and interpretive practices. In other words, meanings in symbolism are assigned by individuals within social contexts, rather than being purely subjective. "The social organization of a particular group helps to shape the world view of the people in it and the types of symbols it produces" (Womack, 2005, p. 37).

In primitive societies, the social hierarchy very much depends on the social power. In an egalitarian society, no one has absolute power over any other. The ability to influence others is based on an individual's personal characteristics, such as the ability to hunt, to heal people, to build alliances, to perform music, or to tell stories (Womack, 2005, p. 52). Symbols serve as tangible units for constructing meaning, circulating through various communication media, and mediating cultural phenomena. They effectively integrate language and practice by connecting the interpreter with the setting and the signifier, or in other terms, the subject, context, and text (Fornäs, 2012, p. 45). However, musical symbols differ significantly from mere object entities. As Douglas R. Hofstadter (1999, p. 622) notes,

> The sounds of music do not refer to serfs or city-states, but they do trigger clouds of emotion in our innermost selves; in that sense musical meaning is dependent on intangible links from the symbols to things in the world-those "things", in this case, being secret software structures in our minds.

William Tallmadge (1962) categorised the communicating meaning through music symbolism into five groups: universal, stylistic, national, private, and verbal. In this section, we benefit from his categorisation to illustrate different levels of communication through music symbolisation.

Universal Music Symbolisations

Universal music symbols in general include pitch, tone quality, rhythm, harmony, melody, sounds of nature, and dynamics. High pitches are perceived as smaller and more feminine, while low pitches are perceived as larger and more masculine. The tone quality can describe a wide range of emotions and feelings. Rhythm can symbolise movement and convey a sense of excitement or relaxation. Harmony can symbolise simplicity or complexity. Melody can symbolise a person or quality and can be weak or strong, curvilinear or angular. Dynamics can symbolise increasing or decreasing excitement or intensity. Moreover, music can imitate natural sounds to symbolise them in a musical context.

Studying musical symbols requires an approach that goes beyond the extremes of universalism and relativism. For instance, two cultures might utilise the same scale but interpret it in fundamentally different ways. Conversely, two cultures might exhibit vastly different musical structures while still adhering to similar underlying principles. This complexity highlights the importance of considering both shared elements and unique interpretations in the study of music across cultures.

Stylistic Music Symbolisations

Stylistic elements such as tonality and mode vary across cultures and historical periods, yet they play a crucial role in defining the musical characteristics of a specific style. Tonality, in particular, is essential for musical communication within that style, as it fosters a sense of movement and resolution. It is believed that the minor mode can evoke seriousness, darkness, sombreness, and sadness, while the major mode symbolises joy, happiness, and optimism for Western-inhabited listeners. We face similar relations between modes and emotions in other cultures. For instance in Arabic music *maqām* "*Rāst*" gives a feeling of masculine love, pride, power, and sound mind, which is used frequently in religious music. While, *maqām* "*Nawā*" gives a feeling of mysticism.

National Music Symbolisations

National symbols convey certain meanings to people within a particular nationality. The national identity is defined as "a form of imaginative identification with the symbols and discourses of the nation-state" (Barker & Galasinski, 2001, p. 124). Street cries, bell tunes, yodelling, folk tunes, national anthems, national dances, and certain musical instruments all lend regional colour to the music performed on them. Scales and idiomatic characteristics also reflect the regions that use them.

In countries formerly known as Yugoslavia, for instance, the cultural landscape varied in every state. In Croatia, the prevailing popular culture found expression in Croatian dance music and "petit-bourgeois," neo-conservative patriotic songs. However, a rough version of this culture manifested among the general populace through war songs steeped in hatred. Meanwhile, in Bosnia, Bosnian Muslim forces cultivate nationalist songs infused with animosity, as well as religious anthems celebrating the Islamic concept of džihad, or holy war. The entertainment scene across the region was notably characterised by a vibrant pop-folk genre, reminiscent of new folk music and Serbian turbo-folk. These songs often featured love lyrics that both celebrated patriarchal values and explored themes of eroticism, while their melodies were heavily influenced by Arabic and Turkish musical traditions (Kronja, 2004).

The diverse musical expressions and cultural symbols of every nation not only highlight the national identity and regional distinctions but also reveal how music serves as a powerful medium for both celebration and conflict, reflecting the complex interplay of history, politics, and collective social values.

Private Music Symbolisations

To fully appreciate the diverse characteristics of national music symbolisations, it is essential to contrast these collective expressions of identity with the more individualised interpretations found in private music symbolisations, where personal connections and specialised knowledge play a critical role in shaping musical experiences.

Private symbols are unique to certain composers or listeners and require familiarity with the symbolism to be understood. In game designing, privet music symbols may be used only in serious games with targeted specialist audiences. These symbols enhance the gaming experience for players who are knowledgeable about music theory, history, or other specific areas. Serious games with music symbols create more challenging and engaging gameplay mechanics for players who are skilled in reading and interpreting music symbols.

Sound symbolisation in music comprises components, such as signs, signals, metaphors, and emotions. In the following section, we give a brief explanation of those components.

Signs and Signals

A sound or combination of sounds, is used to convey a particular meaning or emotion to the listener. Audio signs and audio signals are terms that may be used interchangeably, but they can also have distinct meanings depending on the context in which they are used.

"Sound signals" refers to any type of sound that is used to convey information or communicate a message like alarms, sirens, or warning sounds. "Sound signs," conversely, are mostly utilised in situations where other forms of communication are ineffective, such as in darkness or for individuals who are visually impaired or blind and cannot rely on visual cues. For instance, sound signs in public places such as train stations, airports, or shopping centres help people navigate their surroundings. While sound signs may assign specific things to people of a particular cultural or linguistic group, sound signals are mostly universal and used across different cultures and languages.

Sound signs can be intentional, such as a doorbell ring to indicate someone's presence, or unintentional, such as the sound of footsteps approaching. In the context of communication, audio signals can include spoken language, musical sound, or any other sound used to convey meaning.

An audio signal can take many forms, from a simple beep or tone that signals the completion of a task, to more complex sounds that convey information about a particular event or situation. For example, the sound of a siren can be used as an audio sign to alert people to an emergency, while the sound of a doorbell can be used to signal the arrival of a visitor. In sound signals, the meaning or message conveyed by the sound is often culturally determined and can vary depending on the context in which the sound is used. For example, the sound of a rooster crowing might be used as an audio sign to indicate the start of a new day in some cultures, while in others it might be associated with other meanings or messages.

Moslem call to prayer (adhan) is an example of an audio sign that is culturally determined. The adhan is a melodic Islamic call to worship that is sounded from mosques five times a day to summon Muslims to perform their obligatory prayers. The adhan typically begins with the phrase "Allahu Akbar" (God is the greatest) and includes other phrases. For Muslims, hearing the adhan can evoke a sense of reverence, unity, and connection to their faith and community.

In some Asian cultures, the sound of a gong is used as an audio sign. In many Buddhist and Taoist temples, for example, a large gong is struck at the start and end of each meditation session to signal the beginning and end of the practice or to mark important events or ceremonies. The sound of the gong can help to focus the mind and create a sense of calm and stillness, which is essential for effective meditation.

In video games, sound signs and signals serve as crucial means of challenge. Earcons serve as effective auditory cues to convey critical information to players, particularly through warning signals. For example, a distinct sounds that alert players to a variety of in-game events, such as potential ambushes, calls for allies to attack or defend, or requests for teammates to regroup at a specific location on the battlefield. These sounds function as a blend of notification and warning signals, allowing players to either respond immediately or choose to ignore them depending on the context. While designed to facilitate communication among players, pings are not instinctive sounds; they require prior learning for players to grasp their meanings effectively (Ng & Nesbitt, 2013). These audio elements challenge gamers' perception and reaction times, requiring them to stay alert and utilise their auditory senses strategically.

Serious video games, such as simulations and educational games, often require more realistic and accurate sound signals compared to entertainment video games. This is because serious games aim to replicate real-world scenarios and provide learning experiences for players. As a result, the sound signals in serious video games are typically designed to be more immersive, detailed, and lifelike.

Metaphors

Metaphors in sound symbolism refer to how sounds are used to represent and convey meaning beyond their literal definitions. In speech, a metaphor is a sound figure that uses one thing to represent another thing. The purpose of metaphor is to entertain and divert, and its use always constitutes a deviation from the "plain and strictly appropriate style" (Black, 1954). Simple examples in English are "the clouds are crying" and "the branches are fighting with one another."

Metaphor in speech sometimes associates an imitative or a mimical sound with a particular semantical concept. Nock, tik tok, and shush are examples of the association of sounds to concepts. For example, in many languages, the sounds "sl-" and "sn-" are associated with concepts related to slipperiness and smoothness, like "slip" and "slide" or "snuggle" and "sniff." These sounds are often used metaphorically in words and phrases to communicate these concepts. For instance, in English, we have the phrase "slick as a whistle," which uses the "sl-" sound to create a metaphorical association between smoothness and the sound of a whistle.

We can see numerous links between phonetic aspects and the meaningfulness of sounds and speeches. Once one cannot deliver his/her emotions or meanings in his/her mind, metaphors become very helpful. In this way, metaphors help convey abstract or complex ideas through the use of sound symbolism. Metaphors in sound and speech are different from one culture to another. Common forms of these auditory metaphors include onomatopoeia, phonesthemes, poetic metaphors, and the concepts of euphony and cacophony.

Onomatopoeia

As mentioned above there are verbal and non-verbal speech sounds that come to exist by an imitation of sound effects of the nature or animal sounds they describe. "Buzz" for the sound of a bee, "hiss" for the sound of air or steam escaping, and "sizzle" for the sound of something frying are among the onomatopoeia. Sasamoto (2019) defines onomatopoeia as words that mimic sounds. Other terminologies such as mimetics, expressive, and ideophones are also used to categorise words that fall within this description. For instance, in Hindi "tut" is an imitation of the sound of breaking something and "korako" for the sound of a crow cawing. Indeed, in Japanese "doki" mimics the sound of a heart beating and "mogo" mimics the sound of chewing.

Onomatopoeic verbal or non-verbal speeches often function as metaphors for signifying the things they represent. Onomatopoeia also presents a challenge for de Saussure's theory of language arbitrariness (the assumption that the link between word form and meaning is arbitrary), since the sounds of onomatopoeic words seem to resemble or imitate their interpretations (Sasamoto, 2019). In video games, the sound-mimicking words, such as "swoosh" for a sword swing or "clang" for metal colliding, serve not only as verbal cues but also as auditory representations of actions and events within the game world. Immediate sensory responses are usually used to complement visual elements. For instance, the sound of a character jumping might be represented by the playful "boing," while the thud of a heavy object landing might be conveyed through a deep "thump."

Phonesthemes

Phonesthemes are groups of words that share a common sound in beginnings or endings and related meanings. For instance, many English words beginning with the sound /ex-/ are associated with "out" such as exit, export, exhort, expire, expend, exhale, etc., and /in-/ are associated with "in," such as indoor, inspire, inhale, inside, and import. These words create a metaphorical association between the sound and the concept of "out" and "in." In Russian, the sound "gr-" is often associated with a sense of grandeur or size, as seen in words like grozny (terrible) and grud (breast).

Benjamin K. Bergen (2004) found that common phonaesthemes in English can influence how people think of words, similar to how morphemes do. This suggests that phonaesthemes are meaningful to speakers, both consciously and unconsciously.

Poetic Metaphor

Metaphors are a prevalent and powerful device in poetry and literature. We previously explored the concept of metaphor in this chapter. A metaphor is a figure of speech that draws a comparison between two distinct things or connects a series of words in meaningful ways. "The essence of metaphor is understanding and experiencing one kind of thing in terms of another" (Lakoff & Johnson, 1980, p. 5). It underpins the effectiveness of metaphors in facilitating communication and artistic expression. For example, the phrase "Life is a rollercoaster" illustrates this by likening life to a rollercoaster, highlighting their shared qualities of unpredictability, turbulence, and excitement. In other words, metaphors often use the structure "A is B" or "A resembles B." Metaphors emphasise symbolic connections and should not be interpreted literally. They add layers of depth and meaning that go beyond surface descriptions. "Love is a battlefield" tries to say they are both intense, risky, and require struggle. However, we love to be in love but hate to be on a dangerous war battlefield. Poetic metaphors can give familiar things fresh and thought-provoking perspectives.

Metaphors extend beyond the written word to encompass audiovisual elements, creating multi-layered narratives that resonate with players on emotional and cognitive levels. Hermann Kappelhoff and Sarah Greifenstein (2017) explore the idea of embodied meaning through audiovisual metaphors, emphasising their role in the fictionalisation processes within video games. Eric Zimmerman (2008) introduces a new concept called "gaming literacy," emphasising the importance of three interrelated components: systems, play, and design. This approach reconceptualises how games function within cultural contexts and highlights their potential as tools for fostering critical skills necessary for participation in modern society. By advocating for a playful engagement with systems and the creative processes of design,

Zimmerman argues that gaming literacy can cultivate innovative thinking and problem-solving abilities, thereby redefining what it means to be literate in a rapidly evolving landscape. In video game design, metaphors aim to create surprising and inexhaustive meaning for players. Therefore, metaphors are likely used in independent games which convey strong personal emotions, or in narrative content.

The repetition of certain consonant sounds, known as alliteration, can create a sense of rhythm, mood, or emphasis. In the line "The fair breeze blew, the white foam flew," from Samuel Taylor Coleridge's poem the repeated /f/ and /b/ sounds evoke the feeling of wind and waves, creating a vivid metaphorical image of the sea.

Euphony and Cacophony

Euphony refers to the pleasant, harmonious combination of sounds in a word or phrase, while cacophony denotes a harsh, discordant combination of sounds. For English listeners longer vowels and more sonorous consonants like "l," "m," and "n" are considered to be euphonic. While harsher consonants like "k" or "t" are considered to be cacophonic. These contrasting qualities can be used metaphorically to convey different emotions or atmospheres. For example, the soothing, melodic sounds of words like "lullaby" and "murmur" create a calming effect, while the harsh, abrupt sounds of words like "jagged" and "grating" evoke a sense of discomfort or tension. In African tribal music, the use of drums, bells, and other percussion instruments creates a cacophonous and energetic sound that is used for celebrations and rituals. However, in Celtic music, a combination of flutes, fiddles, and harps creates a sense of euphony because of its beautiful and melodious sound.

In intermedial[1] and transmedial[2] arts, like cinema and video games, sound can be suggested not only by audible elements but also by visual ones. Ling Zhang (2018) calls this phenomenon "metaphoric sound," by which she refers to the sense of rhythm and musicality suggested by camera movement, bodily kinesis, and editing. In this sense "sound" even if not heard, can be imagined through silence which Zhang calls the "ultimate metaphoric sound." It is somehow what we can refer to as audible silence.

> Once you stray into metaphoric sound, which is simply sound that does not match what you are looking at, the human mind will look for deeper and deeper patterns . . . at the geographic level, the natural level, the psychological level . . . the ultimate metaphoric sound is silence.
>
> (Zhang, 2018, p. 278)

For example, in *Berlin: Symphony of a Great City* (1927), one of the most famous examples of city symphony films, the director Walter Ruttmann uses fast cuts, rhythmic patterns, and contrasting images to create a sense of the noise, speed, and energy of Berlin.

Metaphoric sound can also be found in the works of Liu Na'ou,[3] whose use of sound creates a new form of cinematic expression that transcends the limitations of silent film and the conventions of sound film. In his analysis of the interplay between sound and image in film, Liu Na'ou draws a comparison between "light tone" and "acoustic tone" in relation to various cinematic genres and styles. He argued that variations of volume and pitch in acoustic tone are comparable to those of light and shadow in "light tone." Liu proposed a correlation between the pitch of sounds, which he classifies into three categories (high, mid-register, and low) and various film genres and styles (Zhang, 2018, p. 290):

Higher-pitched sounds: These tones should be employed for comedies, to match their faster dialogue and action and depict a brisk, jaunty atmosphere. This sound, however, is not appropriate for serious dramas like tragedies, because it does not match the solemn emotion and atmosphere of such genres.

Middle-pitched sounds: The mid-pitched tone matches melodrama and its sentimental emotional fluctuations, since the versatility of the mid-pitched tone can be used to express and reinforce the sense of life's ups and downs and their alternation between happiness and sadness.

Low-pitched sounds: This category of tones is more appropriate for expressing the restraint and austerity, as well as the deep emotional force of dramas, which attract more serious and quiet audiences.

Even though music and language have several analogies as both benefit from the medium of sound in their communications, when it comes to sensational experience, it is better to compare the sensation of music to the sensation of touch. The tactile model for understanding musical experience provides a new tool with which to treat the perennial debate in music between rational understanding and personal emotions. Music is like touching the self, a touching that gives us information about the modalities of human experience or the dispositions of humans to understand particular situations or life itself in a multitude of possible ways. In this way, music is a way of conveying non-conceptual information about what it is like to experience something in a certain way, similar to how touch can convey information about a person's disposition or inner state.

> *The Aesthetic Metaphor Thesis* suggests that descriptions of music in terms of emotion, motion, and height are almost always metaphorical, and the aesthetic realist maintains that these are metaphorical descriptions of aesthetic properties of music. However, there is a fundamental distinction between aesthetic and nonaesthetic concepts, and possession of the nonaesthetic concept is a partial cause of possession of the aesthetic concept. The causal account suggests that there is a causal relation between the two concepts.
>
> (Zangwill, 2014, pp. 1–2)

In a realistic approach to aesthetic descriptions, music is seen as metaphorical expressions. In such an approach, non-aesthetic words must be used to describe both aesthetic and non-aesthetic aspects of music, and a causal relationship between these concepts must be established. This causal account explains how aesthetic and non-aesthetic concepts are separate but linked.

Emotions

Roberts et al. (2024) investigate the impact of music's emotional content on player behaviour and experience in video games, challenging the traditional focus on simpler musical parameters like tempo. Through a controlled player study involving 36 participants, they distinguish between "peaceful" and "powerful" music, revealing that powerful music significantly enhances player tension and risk-taking behaviours, contrary to earlier assumptions that higher tempo music alone drives these effects. Their findings indicate that emotional content, rather than tempo, plays a pivotal role in shaping players' immersive experiences and decision-making processes during gameplay.

Stephen Davies (1980) presents an analysis of the expression of emotion in music, with a focus on distinguishing between the expression of emotion in music itself and the expression of emotion through music. The expression of emotion in music refers to the ways in which emotions are conveyed and interpreted within the music itself. This can include the use of melody, harmony, rhythm, dynamics, and other musical elements to evoke certain emotions in the listener.

In the context of video game music, this can involve composing music that complements the gameplay experience and enhances the emotional impact of the game. On the other hand, the expression of emotion through music in video games refers to the ways in which music is used as a tool to communicate and convey emotions within the game itself. This can include using music to underscore dramatic moments, heighten tension, create atmosphere, or evoke a specific emotional response from the player. Davies (1980) says that the expression of emotions in music is frequently shaped by a variety of factors, including the composition process, the performance itself, and the dramatic context in which the music is presented. In video games, this dramatic context encompasses the challenges that players encounter at specific moments, as well as the overall progression of dramatic tension throughout the game and the player's condition in those situations.

Affective prosody and emotional vocalisation are two forms of vocal emotions. The affective prosody refers to the tone of voice in speaking, and emotional vocalisation is a term that denotes the vocal expression of emotions without linguistic content and using words, such as laughs, cries and screams. Peretz et al. (2013, p. 296) propose that music and vocal emotions have common acoustic features, such as pitch, loudness, timbre, and contour, that can trigger similar emotional reactions in listeners, and they also activate the same neural mechanisms and pathways that are responsible for perceiving and producing vocal emotions.

Voice acting plays a significant role in conveying emotions, with actors using changes in tone, pitch, and volume to express various emotions. In Japanese video games, emotions in speech may be symbolised through more subtle cues, such as changes in the colour of text or background music, as well as the use of anime-style facial expressions and gestures. Emotions may also be conveyed through the use of specific words or phrases that are associated with certain emotions in Japanese culture. In other cultures, such as Middle Eastern or African cultures, emotions in video games may be symbolised through culture-specific gestures, intonations, and expressions that convey emotions in a particular way unique to that culture.

While human emotions are more or less similar among people of all cultures, the way people of every culture describe and communicate their complex emotional meanings through the use of speech and music differs from one culture to another. Some key differences of expression of emotions between English and Spanish speeches are compared below.

Certain types of music such as opera, ballet, and song are often encumbered by drama, body movements, or words which may be expressive in themselves, making it difficult to claim that emotions may be expressed in music alone. Emotion words retain their meaning in their primary use when applied to music, and musical expressiveness compels emotional responses from us because it reflects and reflects upon the world of emotions.

The emotional resonance of performers' body movements, whether musicians or dancers, can evoke feelings that may not be directly conveyed through the music alone. This includes the movements of both the in-game characters and the body of gamers themselves. As players engage with in-game characters that exhibit vivid emotional gestures, they may find themselves immersed in a complex emotions woven by both visual and auditory stimuli. The concept of mirror neurons suggests that when players witness characters experiencing strong emotions, they may unconsciously mirror those emotions, leading to a shared emotional experience. Karen Collins (2011) asks "Can a videogame make us cry?" Collins explores the relationship between sound design in video games and players' emotional engagement with characters through the lens of embodied cognition. She draws upon the concept of mirror neurons, which facilitate empathetic responses by activating similar neural pathways when one observes actions or emotions in others, including virtual characters. "We may interpret video game characters in anthropomorphic terms, and this anthropomorphism may help us to create an empathic relationship to those characters" (Collins, 2011, p. 80). She argues that sound plays a crucial role in fostering identification and empathy, highlighting how gestural, embodied interactions with sound can enhance emotional depth in gaming experiences.

Many games now feature adaptive audio systems that dynamically adjust based on player actions and emotional states. This creates a feedback loop, allowing the audio to respond to the player's feelings and significantly enhancing emotional engagement. With the continuous advancement of technology, we are witnessing a profound evolution in the ability to evoke gamers' emotions, pushing the boundaries of what we currently experience in gameplay.

Notes

1 Intermediality refers to the relations between different media forms, such as cinema, literature, music, etc.
2 Transmediality refers to the phenomena that transcend the boundaries of a single medium, such as stories, characters, themes, etc.
3 Liu Na'ou (1905–1940) novelist and filmmaker born in Taiwan and worked in Shanghai during the period of Second Sino-Japanese War.

Bibliography

(1894). *Musical Times*, September issue.

Abdo, E. (2022, August 2). Is localizing games into Arabic as difficult as it seems? No. There are solutions. *LinkedIn*. https://www.linkedin.com/pulse/localizing-games-arabic-difficult-seems-solutions-eman-abdo/

Adams, C. R. (1976). Melodic contour typology. *Ethnomusicology*, *20*, 179–215.

Agar, M. (2007). Culture blends. In *A cultural approach to interpersonal communication: Essential readings* (pp. 13–24). Discourse & Society.

Al-Batineh, M., & Alawneh, R. (2021). Translation hacking in Arabic video game localization: The history and current practices. *Translation Spaces*, *10*(2), 202–230.

Alkadi, T. (2010). *Issues in the subtitling and dubbing of English-language films into Arabic: Problems and solutions* [Doctoral dissertation, Durham University].

Allen, A. S., & Dawe, K. (2016). *Current directions in ecomusicology: Music, culture, nature*. Routledge.

Altenmüller, E., Schmidt, S., & Zimmermann, E. (Eds.). (2013). *Evolution of emotional communication: From sounds in nonhuman mammals to speech and music in man*. Oxford University Press.

Amphoux, P. (1993). *L'identité sonore des villes européennes – Tome 1: Techniques d'enquêtes [The sonic identity of European cities – Tome 1: Survey Techniques]*. Centre de Recherche sur l'Espace Sonore et l'Environnement Urbain, École d'Architecture de Grenoble and Lausanne: Institut de Recherche sur l'Environnement Construit, École Polytechnique de Lausanne.

Anıkın, A., Bååth, R., & Persson, T. (2018). Human non-linguistic vocal repertoire: Call types and their meaning. *Journal of Nonverbal Behavior*, *42*, 53–80.

Aronoff, M., & Fudeman, K. (2011). *What is morphology?* (2nd ed.). John Wiley & Sons.

Assmann, J. (1995). Collective memory and cultural identity. *New German Critique*, (65), 125–133.

Australianwznlnc. (2024). *The Didgeridoo: A journey through sound and culture*. https://australian.nativetribe.info/the-didgeridoo-a-journey-through-sound-and-culture-2/

Avery, P., & Ehrlich, S. (1992). *Teaching American English pronunciation*. Oxford University Press.

Azadehfar, M. R. (2008). Impact of Tahrīr in rhythmic structure of Iranian classical music. *Māhūr, Tehran*, *39*, 61–75.

Azar, G., & Drogendijk, R. (2016). Cultural distance, innovation and export performance. *European Business Review*, *28*(2), 176–207.

Azoy, G. W. (1982). *Buzkashi, game and power in Afghanistan*. University of Pennsylvania Press.

Bankieris, K., & Simner, J. (2015). What is the link between synaesthesia and sound symbolism? *Cognition*, *136*, 186–195.

Barker, C., & Galasinski, D. (2001). *Cultural studies and discourse analysis: A dialogue on language and identity*. Sage Publications.

Beaton, R. (1980). Structure of the demotic tradition: Imagery and themes. In *Folk poetry of modern Greece* (pp. 58–73). Cambridge University Press.

Bekoff, M. (2000, October). Animal emotions: Exploring passionate natures: Current interdisciplinary research provides compelling evidence that many animals experience such emotions as joy, fear, love, despair, and grief – we are not alone. *BioScience*, *50*(10), 861–870.

Benjamin, W. (1925–1926). One way street. In *One way street and other writings* (pp. 45–104). Verso.

Benjamin, W. (1928). Marseilles. In P. Demetz (Ed.), *Reflections: Essays, aphorisms, autobiographical writings* (pp. 13–16). Schocken.

Bergen, B. K. (2004). The psychological reality of phonaesthemes. *Language*, *80*(2), 290–311.

Bernal-Merino, M. A. (2020). Key concepts in game localisation quality. In Ł. Bogucki & M. Deckert (Eds.), *The Palgrave handbook of audio-visual translation and media accessibility* (pp. 297–314). Cham, Switzerland: Palgrave Macmillan.

Berndt, A., & Hähnel, T. (2010). Modelling musical dynamics. In *Proceedings of the 5th audio mostly conference: A conference on interaction with sound* (pp. 1–8). Piteå, Sweden. Association for Computing Machinery.

Binesh, T. (Ed.). (1978). *Maqāṣid al-Alḥān [by 'Abd al-Qādir Ibn Ghaibi Marāghī (d. 1435)]* (2nd ed.). Bongah Tarjomeh va Nashr.

Binesh, T. (Ed.). (1987). *Djāmi' al-Alḥān [by 'Abd al-Qādir Ibn Ghaibi Marāghī (d. 1435)]*. Cultural Studies and Research Institute.

Black, M. (1954). Metaphor. *Proceedings of the Aristotelian Society*, New Series, *55*, 273–294.

Blatter, A. (2007). *Revisiting music theory: A guide to the practice*. Routledge.

Bordwell, D., & Thompson, K. (2012). *Film art: An introduction* (10th ed.). New York: McGraw-Hill.

Briefer, E. F., Sypherd, C. C. R., Linhart, P., Leliveld, L. M., Padilla de La Torre, M., Read, E. R., . . . Tallet, C. (2022). Classification of pig calls produced from birth to slaughter according to their emotional valence and context of production. *Scientific Reports*, *12*, 3409.

Brown, P., & Levinson, S. C. (1987). *Politeness: Some universals in language usage* (Vol. 4). Cambridge University Press.

Bull, M., & Back, L. (2020). *The auditory culture reader*. Taylor & Francis.

Burton, T. (Director). (2019). *Dumbo* [Film]. Walt Disney Studios Motion Pictures. (Original work titled *Dumbo*).

Capone, A., & Mey, J. L. (Eds.). (2015). *Interdisciplinary studies in pragmatics, culture and society* (Vol. 4). Springer.

Chandler, H. M., & Deming, S. O. (2011). *The game localization handbook*. Jones & Bartlett Publishers.

Christidis, Y., & Quinton, M. (2016). Exploring the urban mediterranean soundscapes in Cyprus and Malta: A comparative study. *Interference Journal*, Spring Issue, 103–120.

Clark, J. G. (1855). *The Indian mother's lullaby*. S. Brainard's Sons.

Coates, P. (1998). *Nature: Western attitudes since ancient times*. Berkeley, CA: University of California Press.

Colbert, M. N. W. (2021). *Wayback sound machine: Sound through time space and place* [Doctoral dissertation, Universidade NOVA de Lisboa].

Collins, K. (2011). Making gamers cry: Mirror neurons and embodied interaction with game sound. In *Proceedings of the 6th audio mostly conference: A conference on interaction with sound* (pp. 39–46). New York: Association for Computing Machinery.
Cooke, H. (2017). *Djembe in the field: An exploration of the evolution of the djembe habitus and the emergent djembe paradigm within Facebook* [Doctoral dissertation, University of Suffolk and University of Essex].
Cooper, G. W., & Meyer, L. B. (1960). *The rhythmic structure of music*. University of Chicago Press.
Courvoisier, D. M. (1957). *Melodic analysis in the theory curriculum* [M.M. thesis, Indiana University].
Culpeper, J. (2011). *Impoliteness: Using language to cause offence* (Vol. 28). Cambridge University Press.
Ćwiek, A., Fuchs, S., Draxler, C., Asu, E. L., Dediu, D., Hiovain, K., Kawahara, S., Koutalidis, S., Krifka, M., Lippus, P., Lupyan, G., Oh, G. E., Paul, J., Petrone, C., Ridouane, R., Reiter, S., Schümchen, N., Szalontai, Á., Ünal-Logacev, Ö., . . . Perlman, M. (2021). Novel vocalizations are understood across cultures. *Scientific Reports*, *11*(1), 10108.
Davenport, M., & Hannahs, S. J. (2010). *Introducing phonetics and phonology* (3rd ed.). Routledge.
Davies, S. (1980, January). The expression of emotion in music. *Mind*, New Series, *89*(353), 67–86.
Densmore, F. (1918). *Teton Sioux music* (Bulletin 61st ed.). Bureau of American Ethnology.
Di Marco, F. (2007). Cultural localization: Orientation and disorientation in Japanese video games. *Tradumàtica: traducció i tecnologies de la informació i la comunicació*, *5*, 1–12.
During, J. (2010). *Radīf Tār va Setār Mirzā 'Abdullah [Version Nūr 'Ali Brumand]*. Māhūr.
Edgar, A. N. (2019). *Culturally speaking: The rhetoric of voice and identity in a mediated culture*. The Ohio State University Press.
Eelen, G. (2001). *A critique of politeness theories*. St. Jerome Pub.
Fahlenbrach, K. (2016). *Embodied metaphors in film, television, and video games: Cognitive approaches*. Routledge, Taylor & Francis Group.
Farina, A., Buscaino, G., Ceraulo, M., & Pieretti, N. (2014). The soundscape approach for the assessment and conservation of Mediterranean landscapes: Principles and case studies. *Journal of Landscape Ecology*, *7*(1), 10–22.
Feld, S. (1996). Waterfalls of songs: An acoustemology of place resounding in Bosavi, Papua New Guinea. In S. Feld & K. H. Basso (Eds.), *Senses of place* (1st ed., pp. 91–136). School of American Research Advanced Seminar Series. Santa Fe and Seattle: School of American Research Press.
Fernández, I., Carrera, P., Sánchez, F., Paez, D., & Candia, L. (2000). Differences between cultures in emotional verbal and non-verbal reactions. *Psicothema*, *12*(Supp 1), 83–92.
Ferrarini, L., & Scaldaferri, N. (2020). *Sonic ethnography: Identity, heritage and creative research practice in Basilicata, southern Italy*. Manchester University Press.
Finch, G. (2000). *Linguistic terms and concepts*. Macmillan Press Ltd.
Finson, J. W. (1997). *The voices that are gone: Themes in nineteenth-century American popular song*. Oxford University Press.
Fodor, I. (1976). *Film dubbing: phonetic, semiotic, aesthetic and psychological aspects* (1st ed.). Hamburg: Buske.
Fornäs, J. (2012). *Signifying Europe*. Intellect.

Fritsch, M., & Summers, T. (Eds.). (2021). *The Cambridge companion to video game music*. Cambridge University Press.
FWTP. (2025). *Free walking through Peru*. https://freewalkingtoursperu.com/en/blog/10-most-famous-festivities-of-peru/
Gendron, M., Roberson, D., van der Vyver, J. M., & Barrett, L. F. (2014, April). Cultural relativity in perceiving emotion from vocalizations. *Psychological Science, 25*(4), 911–20.
Gibbons, W. (2021). "Open worlds: Globalization, localization and video game music. In *The Cambridge companion to video game music* (pp. 359–375). Cambridge University Press.
Goibnazarov, C. (2017). *Qasīda-khonī a musical expression of identities in Badakhshan, Tajikistan tradition, continuity, and change* [Doctoral dissertation, Humboldt-Universität zu Berlin].
Gottschall, J. (2012). *The storytelling animal: How stories make us human*. Houghton Mifflin Harcourt.
Gough, D. (2017). Re-contextualized carnivals: A Brazilian art form in the global spaces of festivalization. *ASAP/Journal, 2*(1), 199–219.
Hall, E. T. (1959). *The silent language*. A Fawcett Premier Book.
Herzog, G. (1928). The Yuman musical style. *Journal of American Folk-Lore, 41*(160), 183–231.
Herzog, G. (1950). Song. In M. Leach (Ed.), *Funk and Wagnall's standard dictionary of folklore, mythology and legend* (pp. 1032–1050). Funk and Wagnall's.
Hinton, L., Nichols, J., & Ohala, J. J. (Eds.). (2006). *Sound symbolism*. Cambridge University Press.
Hofstadter, D. R. (1999). *Gödel, Escher, Bach: An eternal golden braid*. Basic Books.
Hogan, David. W. (1972). *Men of the sea: Coastal tribes of South Thailand's west coast*. Siam Society.
Holmes, J. (2013). *Women, men and politeness*. Routledge.
Ibn Sīnā. (1992). *Dānish Nāmeh-i 'Alā'ī* (T. Binesh, Ed.). Markaz Nashr Dānishgahi [Iran University Press].
Imai, M., & Kita, S. (2014). The sound symbolism bootstrapping hypothesis for language acquisition and language evolution. *Philosophical Transactions of the Royal Society B: Biological Sciences, 369*(1651), 20130298.
Ivănescu, A. (2021). Pop music, economics and marketing. In T. Summers & M. Fritsch (Eds.), *Cambridge companion for video game music*. Cambridge University Press.
Jaume, A. C., & Coll, E. F. (2019). Music, noise and singing in silence: Industrial soundscape and working experience in the factory. The case of Menorca. *Quadrivium*, (10), 6.
Jeon, J. Y., Hong, J. Y., & Lee, P. J. (2013). Soundwalk approach to identify urban soundscapes individually. *Journal of the Acoustical Society of America, 134*(1), 803–812.
Jiménez-Crespo, M. A. (2013). *Translation and web localization*. New York-London: Routledge.
Jiménez-Crespo, M. A. (2019). Localization. In M. Baker & G. Saldanha (Eds.), *The Encyclopedia of translation studies* (pp. 299–304). New York–London: Routledge.
Johnson, C. I. (1964). Navaho corn grinding songs. *Ethnomusicology, 8*, 101–120.
Jurčević, J. (2019). Sound symbolism of contemporary communication: Croatian imitative expressions in computer-mediated discourse. In *Language, music and computing: Second international workshop, LMAC 2017, St. Petersburg, Russia, April 17–19, 2017, revised selected papers 2* (pp. 91–110). Springer International Publishing.

Kamp, M. (2021). Autoethnography, phenomenology, and hermeneutics. In *The Cambridge companion to video game music* (pp. 159–175). Cambridge University Press.

Kappelhoff, H., & Greifenstein, S. (2017). Metaphorische Interaktion und empathische Verkörperung. Thesen zum filmischen Erfahrungsmodus. *Empathie im Film. Perspektiven der Ästhetischen Theorie, Phänomenologie und Analytischen Philosophie, hrsg. v. Malte Hagener, Ingrid Vendrell Ferran, Bielefeld*, 167–193.

Krause, B. (2015). *Voices of the wild: Animal songs, human din, and the call to save natural soundscapes*. Yale University Press.

Kronja, I. (2004). Turbo folk and dance music in 1990s Serbia: Media, ideology and the production of spectacle. *Anthropology of East Europe Review*, *22*(1), 103–114.

Lakoff, G., & Johnson, M. (1980). The metaphorical structure of the human conceptual system. *Cognitive Science*, *4*(2), 195–208.

Laukka, P., Elfenbein, H. A., Söder, N., Nordström, H., Althoff, J., Iraki, F. K., Rockstuhl, T., & Thingujam, N. (2013). Cross-cultural decoding of positive and negative non-linguistic emotion vocalizations. *Frontiers in Psychology*, *4*, 353.

Leech, G. N. (1983). *Principles of pragmatics*. London and New York: Longman.

Lei, Y., Chi, J., & Huang, M. (2021). Cultural distance and the export of film and TV works: Verification based on China and B&R countries". In *2021 3rd international conference on economic management and cultural industry (ICEMCI 2021)* (pp. 1236–1243). Atlantis Press.

Lerdahl, F., & Jackendoff, R. (1983). *A generative theory of tonal music*. Massachusetts Institute of Technology Press.

Levine, N. G. (2025). Cultural harmony: Bagpipes in Scottish wedding celebrations. *WEZOREE*. https://wezoree.com/inspiration/cultural-harmony-bagpipes-in-scottish-wedding-celebrations/

Lippman, E. A. (1953, October). Symbolism in music. *The Musical Quarterly*, *39*(4), 554–575.

Lipson, A. S., & Brain, R. D. (2009). *Computer and video game law: Cases, statutes, forms, problems and materials*. Carolina Academic Press.

Loisy, A. Firmin. (1921). *Le quatrieme évangile: Les épitres dites de Jean*. Paris: Émile Nourry.

Lomax, A. (1962). Song structure and social structure. *Ethnology*, *1*(4), 425–451.

London, J. (2001). Rhythm. In S. Sadie (Ed.), *The new grove dictionary of music and musicians* (Vol. 21, pp. 227–302). Macmillan Publishers Ltd.

Lorenzen, M. (2007). Internationalization vs. globalization of the film industry. *Industry and Innovation*, *14*(4), 349–357.

Madani, S. (2020, February). 12 distinctive features of Arabic language. *Monthly Magazine Faizan-e Madinah*, pp. 31–33.

Masera, M. (2019). Los símbolos y motivos en la antigua lírica popular hispánica: hacia la construcción de un diccionario. *Boletín de literatura oral*, 229–252.

McAllester, D. P. (1949). *Peyote music* (13th ed.). Viking Fund Publications in Anthropology.

Mendoza, S. A. (2021). Video game localization to Arabic: Challenges and trends. *CCCI*. Retrieved April 2024, from https://ccci.am/.

Merriam, A. P. (1964). The anthropology of music. Bloomington, IN: Northwestern University Press.

Merriam, A. P. (1967). *Ethnomusicology of the flathead Indians. Vol. 44, Fund publications in anthropology*. Aldine.

Mesquita, B., & Frijda, N. H. (1992). Cultural variations in emotions: A review. *Psychological Bulletin*, 112.

Michelmore, G. (2021). Building relationships: The process of creating game music. In M. Fritsch & T. Summers (Eds.), *The Cambridge companion to video game music* (pp. 64–73). Cambridge University Press.
Miller, K. (2007). Jacking the dial: Radio, race, and place in grand theft auto. *Ethnomusicology*, *51*(3), 402–438.
Miller, K. (2012). *Playing along: Digital games, YouTube, and virtual performance*. Oxford University Press.
Mills, S. (2003). *Gender and politeness* (No. 17). Cambridge University Press.
Moonstone, D. (2024). *Australian dreamtime and didgeridoo ceremonies*. https://medium.com/@dmoonstone/australian-dreamtime-and-didgeridoo-ceremonies-af5ae2a91559
Myers, J. (1992). *The way of the pipa: Structure and imagery in Chinese lute music*. Kent State University Press.
Newmark, P. (1991). *About translation* (Series 74). Multilingual Matters Press.
Ng, P., & Nesbitt, K. (2013). Informative sound design in video games. In *Proceedings of the 9th Australasian conference on interactive entertainment: Matters of life and death* (pp. 1–9). Association for Computing Machinery.
Ohata, K. (2004). Phonological differences between Japanese and English: Several potentially problematic. *Language Learning*, *22*, 29–41.
Onar, B. C., & Çatak, G. (2022). Translation and localization of video games: An analysis of uncharted 4 in Turkish. *Connectist: Istanbul University Journal of Communication Sciences*, (62), 91–122.
Ong, W. J. (1967). The presence of the word. *Philosophy and Rhetoric*, *1*(2), 125–128.
Oswalt, R. L. (1994). Inanimate imitatives in English. In *Sound symbolism* (pp. 293–306). Cambridge University Press.
Packman, J. (2010). Singing together/meaning apart: Popular music, participation, and cultural politics in Salvador, Brazil. *Latin American Music Review/Revista de Música Latinoamericana*, *31*(2), 241–267.
Parry, N., & Lane, C. (2005). The memory machine: Sound and memory at the British Museum. *Organised Sound*, *10*(2), 141–148.
Patel, A. D. (2003). Rhythm in language and music: Parallels and differences. *Annals of the New York Academy of Sciences*, *999*(1), 140–143.
Patel, A. D., & Daniele, J. R. (2003). An empirical comparison of rhythm in language and music. *Cognition*, *87*(1), B35–B45.
Peretz, I., Aubé, W., & Armony, J. L. (2013).Towards a neurobiology of musical emotions. The evolution of emotional communication: from sounds in nonhuman mammals to speech and music in man, 277–299.
Pourtorāb, M. K., Alizadeh, H., Oftadeh, M., As'adi, H., Baiani, A., & Fatemi, S. (2012). *Mabānī nazarī va sākhtār-i mūsīqī Irānī [Basics and structure of Iranian music]*. Shrkat chāp va nashr-i ketāb-ha-i darsī.
Putman, D. A. (1985). Music and the metaphor of touch. *The Journal of Aesthetics and Art Criticism*, *44*(1), 59–66.
Pym, A. (2004). Propositions on cross-cultural communication and translation. *Target. International Journal of Translation Studies*, *16*(1), 1–28.
Ramos, A., Lopez, L., Rodriguez, A., Meng, M. T., & Abrams, M. S. (2013). The legal status of video games. *WIPO Report*, *7*.
Roberts, H. H. (1933). *Form in primitive music*. W. W. Norton/American Library of Musicology.
Roberts, J., Wuertz, J., Birk, M. V., Bateman, S., & Rea, D. J. (2024). How the emotional content of music affects player behaviour and experience in video games. In *2024 IEEE gaming, entertainment, and media conference (GEM)* (pp. 1–6). IEEE.

Rothfarb, L. (2002). Energetics. In T. Christensen (Ed.), *The Cambridge history of western music theory* (The Cambridge History of Music, pp. 927–955). Cambridge University Press.
Rovang, S. (2019). *Soundscapes of industrial heritage*. www.sah.org/publications-and-research/fellowship-reports/brooks-fellowship-reports/detail/sah-blog/2019/
Sachs, C. (1953). *Rhythm and tempo: A study in music history*. W.W. Norton.
Sasamoto, R. (2019). *Onomatopoeia and relevance: Communication of impressions via sound*. Springer Nature.
Schafer, R. M. (1977). *The tuning of the world*. Knopf.
Schaffrath, H. (1995). *The Essen Folksong collection in Kern Format*. [Computer database] (D. Huron, Ed.). Center for Computer Assisted Research in the Humanities.
Scherer, K. R. (1979). Nonlinguistic vocal indicators of emotion and psychopathology. In C. E. Izard (Ed.), *Emotions in personality and psychopathology* (pp. 493–529). Plenum.
Slobin, M. (1970). Music and the structure of town life in northern Afghanistan. *Ethnomusicology*, *14*(3), 450–458.
Small, S. (2016). The history of army piping and pipe bands. *RSPBA*, Scotland.
Smits van Waesberghe, J. (1955). *A textbook of melody: A course in functional melodic analysis*. American Institute of Musicology, Miscellaneous 11.
Stanisz, A. (2017). Field recording as method of sonic ethnography. *Arts & Cultural Studies Review*, *1*(31), 1–19.
Stokes, M. (Ed.). (1994). Introduction: Ethnicity, identity, and music. In *Ethnicity, identity, and music: The musical construction of place* (pp. 1–27). Berg.
Szabolesi, B. (1965). *A history of melody*. St. Martin's Press.
Tagg, P. (2011). Caught on the back foot: Epistemic inertia and visible music. *IASPM Journal*, *2*(1–2), 3–18.
Tallmadge, W. (1962). *Symbolic expression in music*. The National Association for Music Education.
Tallman, S., & Fladmoe-Lindquist, K. (2002). Internationalization, globalization, and capability-based strategy. *California Management Review*, *45*(1), 116–135.
Tardieu, J., Magnen, C., Quesada, M. M. C., Spanghero-Gaillard, N., & Gaillard, P. (2015). A method to collect representative samples of urban soundscapes. In *Science and technology for a quiet Europe*. Maastricht, Netherlands: Hal Open Science.
Terpstra, V., & Sarathy, R. (2000). *International marketing*. The Dryden Press.
Tonkiss, F. (2020). Aural postcards: Sound, memory and the city. In *The auditory culture reader* (pp. 243–247). Routledge.
Trehub, S. E., Bull, D., & Thorpe, L. A. (1984). Infants' perception of melodies: The role of melodic contour. *Child Development*, 821–830.
Ullman, S. (1962). *Semantics: An introduction to the science of meaning*. Basil Blackwell.
Wang, T., Wichmann, S., Xia, Q., & Ran, Q. (2023). Temperature shapes language sonority: Revalidation from a large dataset. *PNAS Nexus*, 2(12).
Watts, R. J. (2003). *Politeness*. Cambridge University Press.
Watts, R. J., & Morrissey, F. A. (2019). *Language the singer and the song: The sociolinguistics of folk performance*. Cambridge University Press.
Wierzbicka, A. (2015). Language, and cultural scripts. In *The Routledge handbook of language and culture*. Routledge.
Womack, M. (2005). *Symbols and meaning: A concise introduction*. Rowman Altamira.
Wrench, J. S., Punyanunt-Carter, N. M., & Thweatt, K. S. (2020). *Interpersonal communication: A mindful approach to relationships*. Milne Open Textbooks.

Zangwill, N. (2014, Winter). Music, metaphor, and aesthetic concepts. *The Journal of Aesthetics and Art Criticism*, 72(1), 1–11.

Zhang, L. (2018). Rhythmic movement, metaphoric sound, and transcultural transmediality: Liu Na'ou and the man who has a camera. In *Early film culture in Hong Kong, Taiwan, and Republican China: Kaleidoscopic histories* (pp. 277–301). University of Michigan Press.

Zimmerman, E. (2008). Gaming literacy: Game design as a model for literacy in the twenty-first century. In *The video game theory reader* (pp. 23–32). Routledge.

Zuckerkandl, V. (1956). *Sound and symbol: Music and the external world* (W. R. Trask, Trans.). Pantheon Books.

Index

Note: Page locators in **bold** indicate a table. Page locators in *italics* indicate a figure

For Product Safety Concerns and Information please contact our EU representative GPSR@taylorandfrancis.com Taylor & Francis Verlag GmbH, Kaufingerstraße 24, 80331 München, Germany